Karl Johaentges · Jackie Blackwood

Pictures from New Zealand

CRAIG
POTTON
PUBLISHING

Published in 1997 by Craig Potton Publishing
Box 555, Nelson, New Zealand

Design & calligraphy: Karl Johaentges
Photography: Karl Johaentges
Text: Jackie Blackwood
Colour Separations: ScanKo, Hanover
Typeset: types. Fotosatz, Hanover
Printer: Druckhaus EA Quensen, Lamspringe

First published in Germany 1995 by KaJo
© Edition KaJo bei Stürtz

Printed in Germany
ISBN 0-908802-26-9

LEICA - Foto

Front cover: Mt Tasman, Mt Cook and the
Southern Alps
Sperm whale, Kaikoura coast
Maori couple, Waitangi
Gillespies Beach
Back cover: Walking the Caples Track

Foreword

"Seeing ourselves as others see us" a Kiwi would say of this book. We, the others, are a German photographer and an Australian writer based in Hanover, Germany. Karl Johaentges was first in New Zealand in 1983 when he worked for the Wellington architect Ian Athfield, and we returned together in 1986 to tour and photograph for our first book project as a team. We, like other visitors, came for the great outdoors and to explore a little in nature's playground.

New Zealand has come of age since 1986. In Europe it is no longer in danger of being omitted from world maps, it features in the international media after volcanic eruptions, and recently its economy has been described as an example to other nations. Nine years after our first visit together, we went back, flying halfway around the globe with pounding hearts and great expectations to revisit old friends and places. And despite the escalating visitor numbers that had occurred, we weren't disappointed. Of course in popular places such as Queenstown and Rotorua, more numbers of tour buses than ever emptied their loads into souvenir shops selling sheepskins, woollen socks, carved kiwis and such items (for its thermal wonders everybody must go to Rotorua at least once!)

Another massive and obvious development was the one that had occurred in the Kiwi kitchen. In our first book *New Zealand* (which we dared only to publish in a German edition) we joked with mean pleasure about the colourless Kiwi meals, and the three standard cheddar cheeses: mild, tasty and extra tasty. However, our friends 'down under' are well on their way to overtaking our European gourmet standards. Even in small towns today you can find a café with several sorts of delicious quiches, organic salads and cappuccino on the menu. Still, it's a little sad to discover the old tea rooms (that often served terrible pies but good English tea) disappearing, probably due to people like ourselves.

Visitors can't help comparing New Zealand with landscapes 'back home': a mixture of Swiss Alps, Norwegian fiords, Australian beaches… Such varying landscapes within such a small space attracts many nationalities to its shores. On both our New Zealand journeys we let ourselves be led, following coincidences, invitations, and surprises along the roadside. They were journeys off the beaten tracks, away from the places featured in promotional brochures.

With the images and travel journal that resulted we now want to take the reader off the wide roads in the travel guides. Discovering New Zealand for yourself is of course the best way, but we hope you can make yourself comfortable and join us on our journey, tramping through the rainforests, along deserted beaches and across volcanic plateaus in a little piece of paradise. Without aiming to be complete we have tried to convey something of these South Pacific islands from the eyes of a visitor, relating to the reader some of the coincidental, spontaneous and partly planned experiences we had. Above all it is a visual impression of a land with so many extremes and superlatives it is often difficult to describe in words. Our illustrated narrative is neither adventure tale nor guidebook. We simply want to introduce you to landscapes and life 'at the other end of the world' and bring you closer to events and people travellers may not have had the opportunity to meet: musterers in the Garvie Mountains, the chopper boys in Fiordland, Hundertwasser, the Bay of Islands artist or the Maori Rastafarians from East Cape.

Finally, there's one thing we wish to point out: our travelogue begins in the North Island and ends where we Europeans made first contact with New Zealand's first inhabitants on the northernmost point of the South Island. The photographic journey begins with the mountain Aoraki, the cloud piercer, New Zealand's highest peak and mountain of great spiritual significance, and it ends on the northernmost point of the North Island, Cape Reinga. This is deliberate. We offer two independent journeys – enjoy both!

Jackie Blackwood & Karl Johaentges

3

Carved by glaciers, Dusky Sound, Fiordland National Park

Journey to the Antipodes

Our New Zealand experience began before we even set foot in the country, at 12,000 metres above Hawaii. In-flight video screens on the Air New Zealand plane flickered with images of thermal pools, flightless birds, waterfalls and glaciers-nature in abundance. Tanned and smiling flight attendants served prize-winning New Zealand wines, and asked if we would prefer "fush or chucken" for dinner. We, like other Europeans in the plane, were escaping winter, crowded autobahns and commuter trains, longing feverishly for the great outdoors at the other end of the world, away from pollution and social ills.

Our neighbours in row forty-eight were from Invercargill, a city on the southern point of New Zealand. They had a four week package tour of Europe behind them, and were in raptures over the museums and Metro in Paris, the autobahn and Hofbrauhaus in Munich. In Los Angeles more New Zealanders joined the flight. Most were families laden with Disneyland paraphernalia – the kids wore Mickey Mouse ears, and dads wore Las Vegas T-shirts. For them it's been their getaway holiday from isolation in the South Pacific.

Eight years earlier we made this same long journey to New Zealand and I distinctly recall our arrival in Wellington. After years of conversing in German I had been longing to revert to my mother tongue.

We had no sooner heaved our thirty kilogram backpacks alongside the LPG gas cylinder in the back of the Holden taxi when the greying driver asked the ritual question: "Where do you come from?". His accent immediately gave him away and we reverted to German. By the time we reached the second traffic lights, Michael, the taxi driver, was telling us a classic immigrant's story – his flight from a German-speaking corner of Romania, the post-war

Taxi driver Michael, private photo selection

5

years in Europe and the long sea voyage to the other side of the globe.

Eventually we arrived in the inner city. There! Next to the old parliamentary building Michael showed us the sandwich bar he worked in where the Prime Minister had stood with others to wolf down a pie. And we listened with amusement to the story of a Pomeranian dog that "hatched" an egg, followed by another unbelievable hunting story. At every red light Michael pulled out well-thumbed family snapshots and yellowed newspaper articles from various cavities of his old Holden. Photos of his house and his weekend holiday house, or "bach", spoke of fulfilled dreams in his new homeland.

This time, in 1994, we arrived in Auckland. I felt humbled when I learned that the airport there was named after Jean Batten, a 26-year-old New Zealander who in 1936 had set a new record for flying solo from Britain to New Zealand. The journey took her eleven days in the timber and canvas *Vega Gull*. And here we were, 400 of us, moaning after four movies, five meals and just thirty hours' flying.

We spent out first night at the Ascot Parnell, a small guesthouse in the suburb of Parnell. The owners, Bart and Therese, were newcomers from Holland. Bart, once a successful computer expert, had left his world of bits and bytes to come and serve wonderful breakfasts of muesli, fruit, yoghurt and strong coffee.

What to do when one disembarks numb, dizzy and dazzled from a thirty hour jumbo flight? On our second day in New Zealand we escaped the big city crush of Auckland to look for quiet, and we found it just forty kilometres from New Zealand's largest city, on the west coast. The one hour drive through the beautiful forested Waitakere Ranges gave us what the tour brochures and the in-flight video had promised: nature in abundance.

Here, on Auckland's magnificent west coast the unforgettable beach scenes from Jane Campion's *The Piano* were filmed. Our eyes automatically scanned the beach for a piano, but we knew of course that it sank in

the ocean at the end of the film. Our first attempt to swim exposed us as "loopies", an expression for tourists (maybe because we do a loop tour and leave?). Like polar bears in a coal mine, our white winter skin was a dazzling white against the black volcanic sands of the beach. Coloured flags indicated safe swimming areas, but we didn't have the courage, or the surfboards, to fall into the mountainous waves of the Tasman Sea that Auckland surfers love. On top of that yesterday's newspaper had reported freak waves that had suddenly surged in from the turbulent Tasman Sea, washing fishermen from the rocks and surprising surfers. The previous weekend life guards rescued forty-nine people from the water. Last summer there were 1,200 rescue operations.

Instead of going swimming we decided to drive forty kilometres further north to Muriwai Beach. The fifty-kilometre long black ironsand beach is known for the rare mainland gannet (takapu) colony on its cliffs and rock stacks. And even though some nests of the 1,000 pairs of takapu are within a few metres of a viewing platform, these wonderful aerodynamic gliders behave as if we didn't exist at all.

Back in Auckland. January is a hot summer month in the Southern Hemisphere and new arrivals are conspicuous with their lobster-red faces. The well-informed wear wide straw hats. Experts believe that the ozone hole above New Zealand is no larger than the hole above northern Europe, but what's different here is that the air is cleaner. Our slight protection from the ultraviolet rays in Germany (a horrible irony) is Europe's layer of air pollution.

Auckland lies on an isthmus. Maps show the city straddling the narrow neck of land between Waitemata Harbour and the Pacific Ocean in the east, and the wide Manakau Harbour and the Tasman Sea in the west. "Cosmopolitan" Auckland is without doubt queen of the country, a San Francisco of the South Pacific. A quarter of New Zealand's population live within a fifty-kilometre radius of the city, as many people as on the South Island. They are attracted to Auckland by jobs, sunshine, mild winters, and fabulous sport and outdoor possibilities.

Auckland's bays are the home to 70,000 sailing and motorcraft; one in four households are said to own a floating tub in the so called "City of Sails".

The last Monday in January is a holiday originally set aside to celebrate the founding of Auckland in 1841 by Governor Hobson. These days the date is a celebration of wind when the *Anniversary Day Regatta* is held. Over a thousand boats compete in forty classes, leaving the harbour spattered with sails. During this particular January, in 1994, another sailing event had grabbed Auckland's attention, the *Whitbread Round-the-World Yacht Race*. The first of the high-tech yachts were expected at midnight on January 24 and jeeps, Jags, campervans and buses lined all the roads within view of the harbour. Tens of thousands waited along the quayside into the early morning hours for "their" yacht, the local racing yacht *Endeavour*, which was welcomed home with frenzied applause and hooting. She did of course take the lead from the yacht *Tokio* in a spectacular finish.

Berthed at Princess Wharf, the overseas dock, was the *Queen Elizabeth II*, the world's largest cruise ship, which even loomed above the Ferry Building where we were to meet for a seafood lunch. While its 1,800 passengers strolled through the shopping arcades, hundreds of curious onlookers gathered at the ferry pier. Lunchtime joggers slalomed through the swarms in Queen Street. Auckland's main street is anything but royal, (airline and souvenir shops) and some New Zealanders get claustrophobic just at the thought of it. Years ago there was

an attempt to separate pedestrians by painting a line down the pavement, but most Kiwis have adapted to the crowds. This objection to crowds is surprising, but in fact New Zealand is one of the most urban societies on earth, with only fourteen per cent of its population living in rural areas and an even smaller number working in agriculture.

So while most New Zealanders drive through congested traffic to work in offices or factories, the image of a "good keen bloke," the sheep shearer in shorts and rubber boots and a navy blue singlet or checked woollen shirt, is unshakeable. It's

only on weekends or in the summer holidays (from Christmas until the end of January) when cityites don their shorts and escape with their families to the mountains and national parks, or go to their seaside baches. Very few wear red-checked woollen shirts!

"Antipodes" stems from a Greek word "antipous" meaning "opposite feet". Not so long ago in Europe the image of Kiwis down under was still one of a puritan and conservative people. Australians affectionately called them "country cousins". Even the bird after which New Zealanders call themselves is not such a pretty picture –

Auckland – "City of Sails"

a round, half-blind, flightless night creature. But any fear New Zealanders may have had of falling off the edge of the world map before anyone takes notice has long gone. New Zealanders are a confident and independent people. They survived the economic crises of the 1980s and can now sit back and observe we Europeans trying to crawl from our economic slump.

Nevertheless, driven by the limited opportunities in their isolated South Pacific home, more Kiwis leave their homeland than new arrivals squeeze through the narrow door of the immigration department. "No future?" It is mostly young New Zealanders, the up-and-coming academics,

musicians, designers and scientists who try their luck overseas in Australia, Great Britain and Asia. A country with a population of 3.5 million people and 60 million sheep can't promise careers or big money for everyone.

Auckland was the nation's "capital" for a few years. During whaling days last century the capital was located at Russell in the Bay of Islands, then a wild and rollicking metropolis. But after the Crown's representative, Governor William Hobson, persuaded forty Maori chiefs to sign the Treaty of Waitangi in 1840 and enter the Commonwealth, the capital was moved first to Auckland, then in 1865 to Wellington in the centre of the country.

The discovery of gold on the South Island may have also influenced the relocation.

For the rival Maori tribes in the north, Auckland's natural harbour, with its wide branching bays, had been an object of contention for centuries. This is borne out by the Maori name of the harbour: Tamaki makau rau, "Place of a hundred lovers". In 1841 Governor Hobson bought the isthmus for a bargain of £56 in gold, axes, pots, blankets, tobacco and pipes, and he even added a sack of flour and sugar.

Today Auckland is a fascinating multicultural melting-pot of Polynesians, Indians, Chinese, Maori and Pakeha (whites) of all nations. The acute shortage of labourers after World War II, attracted Pacific people in droves. Pacific Islanders sent their savings back home, and the money brought relatives to New Zealand. An oft quoted statistic is that 82 per cent of the population of Niue live in New Zealand and only 18 per cent live on their island. In total the number of Polynesians in New Zealand comprises about 4 per cent of the population. Two-thirds, that is 80,000 Pacific islanders live in Auckland. With its 99,000 Maori, Auckland has become the world's largest Polynesian city.

Karangahape Road, at the southern end of Queen Street, is the city's "Broadway" for people from Tonga, Fiji, Samoa and Cook Islands. Fresh papayas, mangos, bananas and kumara (sweet potato), decorate tiny vegetable shops jammed between airline agencies, strip joints and restaurants. At an Indian grocery store we stood in line for our supplies of curry powder and basmati rice. At lunchtimes young locals gather in the

Luxury ocean-liner QE II in Auckland

Verona Café, which is decorated with a collection of kitsch from the 1960s including an impressive number of bright-orange flower vases.

On weekdays in K-Road, colourful, generous matrons draped in hibiscus-patterned cloth shop for South Sea ingredients. Across the road pubs are filled with marathon drinkers, and in the side streets Pacific Island churches are found in converted warehouses and cinemas. Christian Polynesians seem to take their religion more seriously than the descendants of the missionaries themselves. The *Ekalesia Faapotopotoga Congregational Church of Jesus* is a renovated old cinema, converted into a house of God. On Sunday mornings, crammed cars discharged, to my surprise, as many men as women. The women wore white or bright floral patterns, topped with extravagant wide-brimmed summer hats. Eventually the Minister arrived, a whale of a man dressed in jacket and tie, white shirt tucked into his sarong and his feet exposed in yellow plastic sandals. Elderly Polynesian women will sometimes attend church twice on Sundays. Dressed in their bright white Sunday best, and singing South Pacific melodies the worshippers enliven the dark stuffy hall. For a few hours they can forget the unemployment, money problems and the monotony of factory work and enter another world.

High unemployment amongst Polynesians is a flammable social and ethnic subject, and racism cannot be ignored even in New Zealand. However, compared with many countries, New Zealand is a positive example of racial integration. I don't know of another country where marriage between partners of different races (with contrary colonial backgrounds) is undertaken with so few problems.

History has shown that the social climate of these islands is milder than those in other countries. In the isolated South Pacific the Antipodean colony developed more equality than the society the immigrants had left behind. It is certainly no coincidence that in 1877 this nation of do-it-yourself individualists introduced compulsory education for children of all races. In 1879 all adult males (Pakeha and Maori) had the right to vote, and in 1890, (second after the State of Wyoming, USA) women were given the right to vote. Laws on social welfare were also passed earlier than anywhere else.

A trip into the past

Some 200 years ago these evergreen Southern Hemisphere islands were still unknown to most Europeans. In 1642 the Dutchman, Abel Tasman, searching for the legendary great southern land *Terra australis incognita*, sailed as far as latitude forty-nine degrees south. Then he turned eastwards and discovered *Van Diemens Land* (today Tasmania), and in the same year on December 13 sighted "a great high land", sailing along its stormy west coast to the northern point of the South Island. Believing it to be an enormous continent connected with South America, he named it *Staten Landt*. As others would prove, there was no connection, and the land was eventually rechristened *Niew Zeeland*.

The British explorer, James Cook, kept the name when he anchored the barque *Endeavour* in 1769 in Poverty Bay, south of where Gisborne is today. He was the first recorded European to go ashore in Aotearoa, the "land of the long white cloud." The inhabitants named the white Europeans Pakeha, which roughly means "white skin". The indigenous people named themselves Maori, "the originals", to differentiate themselves from the newcomers.

The ancestors of Maori arrived in double-hulled canoes from Eastern Polynesia about 800 years earlier. Historians believe several waves of immigration occurred until the fifteenth century. Legends tell of "seven canoes" to which every Maori traces his or her ancestry. They arrived in an isolated paradise of plants and birds with only two mammal species, both of them quite inconspicuous bats.

Some decades after Cook's landing the first white settlers began to arrive. First came the whalers, then the traders, followed by liquor dealers and the missionaries. The whaling station, Kororareka, later named Russell, had a reputation in those days as being the "hell hole of the Pacific."

More waves of colonial settlers transformed the once peaceful trading between the Maori and the Pakeha into hate and war. In February 1840 in the Bay of Islands hundreds of Maori, including many chiefs, gathered in front of the British Residence at Russell, agitated and on the verge of rebellion. Pakeha were settling throughout their land, and they foresaw the loss of their dignity, their land and way of life. What could they do? Was it too late, after all these years, to drive the white men by force from their land? Was it possible against their powerful fire weapons? Were not trade and peace the best solution? Didn't the faith of these Christians sound just and sensible?

On the February 6, 1840, at Waitangi, representatives of the Crown in starched uniforms sat opposite Maori chiefs in their flax clothing and feathered cloaks. Forty chiefs put their mark on a sheet of paper, thereby agreeing to the annexation of New Zealand to the British Empire. Now they were "equal members" of the Commonwealth. This bond with Queen Victoria promised Maori that all the land, forests and coastal waters that were still in their possession, would remain theirs, and that only the Crown's representatives were able to purchase land from them. In practice the Pakeha didn't abide by the agreement. Most settlers laughed at this contract with "naked wild men", and the taking of their land was slowed just a little. By 1860 settlers had overtaken the Maori in numbers, and by 1892 two-thirds of the North Island belonged to European immigrants.

When the fate of the Maori is compared with that of the American Indians or Australian Aborigines, this colonisation by treaty (even though it wasn't often complied with) was a major step forward. But from the start the treaty was subject to differing interpretations of concepts such as "ownership" and "landowner."

For over 150 years New Zealanders have been attempting to redefine the treaty. In 1975 the Minister of Maori Affairs, Matiu Rata, introduced a bill that established an independent government commission, the Waitangi Tribunal, to examine all claims of illegally confiscated land. The tribunal has since made spectacular and controversial decisions to the Maori's advantage, and as a result fishing rights and land have been returned to the tribes.

The Maori were never extremely peaceful people. There were many battles between tribes, prisoners were taken as slaves or sometimes eaten, but as long as the battles were carried out with stone cudgels and wooden clubs they were without great consequence. Only after settlers supplied the northern tribes with guns was the bloodshed more significant. Some tribes even marched south to clear old debts. Alcohol, infectious diseases and the rage of the government troops escalated the loss of life. By 1900 the Maori population had shrunk from 140,000 to 40,000. One hundred and fifty-seven years after the Treaty of Waitangi, the Waitangi Day anniversary on February 6 still focuses attention on the country's colonial history. While the white population celebrate the day as the founding of their nation, for many Maori it remains a day of terrible defeat.

The Bay of Islands, with 800 kilometres of coastline, 150 islands and countless bays, always enticed people. Kupe, the mythical Maori voyager from ancestral Hawaiki is supposed to have landed here in his new home, Aotearoa. Captain Cook also drop-

Maori Carving, Auckland War Memorial Museum

ped anchor in its sheltered bays. It was to become the first base for the settlement of New Zealand.

Here in the north, an Austrian, Friedensreich Hundertwasser, today a New Zealander, decided the national flag needed a new design and the Kiwis a new identity symbol. His alternative flag flutters in front of his house and on the *Regentag*, the old retired Sicilian salt ship that brought the artist to the Antipodes. He believes a curled fern frond, bush-green on a white background is an appropriate alternative to the present national flag incorporating Britain's Union Jack.

"The flag symbolises the old and the new, history and progress at the same time", he wrote "like an uncurling fern frond, like a wave of nature, like an unfolding flag. It is the symbol of a growing nation, representing the Maori tradition ... the green of the land ... it is a true ambassador of New Zealand to the world."

His flag flies in front of trendy restaurants and tourist shops, but whether he can convince everyone with his idea is uncertain, although given that Australia is considering a new flag the chances shouldn't be too bad. There's little difference between the flags of Australia and New Zealand anyway. Both have a Union Jack and the Southern Cross on a blue background, they differ only in the number of the stars, six for Australia and four for New Zealand.

It is surprising that more Kiwis haven't thought about the fern motif themselves. It seems an obvious symbol that has been associated with New Zealanders for years.

Kiwi soldiers in the First World War were known to their allies as "Tommy Fernleaf". The export market sells goods labelled with the fern leaf, the national airline flies under a fern frond emblem. The Maori have used the "koru" fern motif for decoration throughout their history. In their jade and wood carving and in the art of the "moko", facial tattooing, forty-five variations of the spiral motif are known.

"A new flag? Impossible!" was the reaction of a war veteran when we showed him the flag on Anzac Day in Kaitaia. (Anzac is an acronym for the Australia New Zealand Army Corp). "We defended the Commonwealth under the flag, too many of us lost lives under the Union Jack." His war medals jingled as he shook with emotion, "You can't just abolish it!" Maybe this memorial day for fallen soldiers was too emotionally charged for such a question to be asked of New Zealand's senior citizens.

The number of stone war memorials in even the smallest towns seemed puzzling in a peaceful country so distant from any battlefields. But New Zealand lost more soldiers per head of population in both World Wars than did Mother England who had called them up. Up till the First World War few New Zealanders ever left their country, and then suddenly they were hurrying in droves to Europe as soldiers. Many considered the journey to war a welcome overseas adventure. Anzac Day is a national holiday in New Zealand to commemorate those killed in the World Wars and particularly those who fell in the battle at Gallipoli. On April 25, 1915 almost the entire Anzac force

was sent to a peninsula in the Dardenelles in a suicidal attack against the Turkish army and completely blown to bits. Ted Weaver, a gunner in the Royal Marines, looked into space as he said "Under my shield it poured shrapnel. I watched them all leave the boats to be massacred." On that day 8,587 Anzac soldiers fell, and 25,000 returned wounded. New Zealanders against the Turks. Which of them knew where their enemy's country was? War craziness "at its best" is portrayed in Peter Weir's moving Australian film *Gallipoli*.

Northland

On the long lonely road from Kaitaia towards Cape Reinga, the settlement Te Kao is hardly noticeable except for a small timber church belonging to a sect of Christian Maori. It's minarets are crowned with a star and a crescent moon, Arepa and Omeka, which stems from the Greek, alpha and omega, beginning and end. In 1918, Tuhupotiki, after experiencing a vision, declared himself a medium of God, preached against his people's native superstitions, and attempted to convert them to a blend of Christianity and Jehovah. Ratana, a small town twenty-three kilometres southeast of Wanganui, soon became a place of pilgrimage and the faith became known as the Ratana faith. Today Ratana is a religious movement that unites many Maori despite their traditional tribal differences.

In 1986 we met a lovely lady, Kerewai Conrad, in Te Kaha. She taught weaving to school children and unemployed women and produced baskets for souvenir shops in Auckland. "Basket weaving is a woman's craft amongst Maori, but these days young Maori women show no interest. They'd rather smoke cigarettes," complained Kerewai, "it's the white Pakeha women that want to learn the flax weaving or to go shopping in Auckland with one of our baskets. Our girls prefer the plastic bags from the supermarkets." With lively sparkling eyes she explained to us the art of weaving with flax and pingao grass that grows here in the northern dunes.

The flax trade was once a flourishing industry in New Zealand. James Cook's botanist, Joseph Banks, obviously impressed by Maori skills, named the sword-shaped fibrous plant, *Phormium tenax*, which means strong basket. From over a hundred varieties of flax, the flax found in New Zealand and in Norfolk Island is extra strong, and was in great demand amongst traders for ropemaking in the early years of the settlement.

One hundred and sixteen kilometres north of Kaitaia the unsealed road came to an end. We had reached Cape Reinga, New Zealand's northernmost point. From the lighthouse, it's possible to watch the Pacific swell colliding with rollers coming in from the Tasman Sea. A signpost gives the directions and distances to the Equator, Sydney, London, Panama and Suva, and the feeling that this is the edge of the world is unshakeable.

Reinga means underworld. To the Maori the Cape is the end of the earthly world. Here, the spirits of the deceased begin their journey back to their original spiritual homeland, Hawaiki, somewhere in Polynesia. The spiritual journey supposedly begins after sunset in the roots of an ancient Pohutukawa tree that leans from the steep cliff above the surging ocean. The spirits arrive along Ninety Mile Beach, and at a small river crossing have the chance to decide whether to return to the dying body or to depart forever.

We had more earthly problems. Karl is the type who fills the petrol tank only when it's nearly empty, and although he knew that petrol pumps were scarce in the Far North, he miscalculated how much fuel we would need. And so we left the Cape with a flickering red fuel tank light with at least fifty kilometres in front of us, wondering where we would come to a standstill. To save petrol, Karl switched the motor off on every hillcrest and crash-started it again after we'd rolled downhill.

We drove on in silence, I because I was annoyed and Karl because he probably thought every wasted word would raise the petrol usage. On the radio all we could receive was a weak signal from a regional radio programme, broadcasting horse racing of all things, live from the course. The commentator's voice was a monotonous litany of unintelligible word staccato, without any intonation.

Horse races are found all over the world, and in New Zealand, it's a multi-million dollar business. There are seventy-one race courses for 3.5 million Kiwis, and they gamble $800 million every year on horses. At the racecourse, the ranks of nervous passionate spectators judge their chances by horse lengths, and tens of thousands of fans from Invercargill to Kaitaia turn up the radio volume. With bets placed at the official TAB office (or with illegal bookies) all hang on every galloping word from the commentator over the loudspeaker. Just short of the finish, a speedy gush and tumble of words rises from the commentator until the winner is clear, and both commentator and horse slow down again. It was a bit like our driving technique.

Heading for Coromandel

The Waikato region south of Auckland is horse country. Its mild climate and fertile fields present ideal breeding conditions, and the wide sandy beaches on Waikato's west coast are a natural training ground for yearlings. Once a year the racing community gathers at Karaka for the yearling sales, hoping to purchase tomorrow's winners. When we went 180 racehorses were sold for more than $10 million on the first day of the two-day auction.

Despite or because of his twenty-three years of age, the breeding stallion Sir Tristram, from a Cambridge stud, was the superstar. The pensioner was said to have mated with eighty-five mares in 1993,

seventy four of which had foals. Such virility draws crowds. Sir Tristram's offspring attain top prices of around $270,000.

New Zealand's reputation as a horse breeders' eldorado began in 1929. The stallion, Phar Lap, which was bought by a clever Australian, became one of the most successful racehorses ever. Long after his mysterious death in America he is still considered a legend. In 1990, when the mare, Kiwi, an outsider, won the Melbourne Cup with a dramatic final sprint, the then unknown breeder and horse became nation-

al heroes overnight. From nowhere they had thrashed stables worth millions of dollars. Now, about four-fifths of the bidders at the sales are Australians, easily recognisable in their William's hats and boots. When Horlicks, another New Zealand horse, won the 1989 Japan Cup, Japanese and Chinese began flying over to buy all female relations of Horlicks. But do the Asians know that he's named after a bedtime drink? Yawn!

Sixty kilometres south of Auckland, we turned eastwards onto a country road

towards Thames and the Coromandel Peninsula. When gold was discovered in 1867, fortune hunters came to Coromandel in droves, including Americans, Australians, and Chinese. Settlements grew here and around the threads of gold throughout early New Zealand pioneer history in Otago, West Coast and Coromandel. The yellow metal was of little use (and therefore little interest) to the Maori. They valued instead a precious green jade-like stone they called pounamu, fighting battles and making long expeditions to the South Island's West Coast to gain access to it.

Thames is one of those places gold put on the map overnight, and left to peaceful insignificance some years later. Of the hundred hotels from those days, six have survived. Just before sunset we drove to the pass above Coromandel Harbour to view the bay. Surrounded by perfectly still water coloured by a red sunset glow, the bay's many tiny rounded islands were spread before our feet like a bowl of melting marshmallows in raspberry jelly. In the distance the tiny lights of metropolitan Auckland had begun to flicker. Having a campervan allowed us to stay overnight in a small parking place above the bay. For dinner we ate fresh perch, cauliflower and boiled salted potatoes and a butter sauce, and for dessert Hokey Pokey ice cream!

Once the peninsula's mountain ridges were covered in dense forests. An army of loggers felled the giant trees, floated them down dammed rivers to the coast, and left cleared areas as grazing land for farmers. Ironically the peninsula is named after the

HMS Coromandel, a freighter that shipped kauri and other native timbers.

Today Coromandel is home to artists, weavers, carvers, conservationists and other creative souls, often living in self-built timber homes or in communes hidden in the bushland. The mild winterless climate, the seclusion and the half day drive to metropolitan Auckland make the peninsula an attractive place to live.

Beyond the small town of Coromandel, familiarly known as Coro, (Kiwis love to shorten names) the tar-sealed road became poorer until beyond Colville it disappeared altogether. Signs warn of the lack of petrol pumps, and for rental cars these days the road to Cape Colville ends in Colville. Gnarled and twisted pohutukawa trees bow like a living portal over the ever narrowing and bumpier coastal road. We have to be satisfied with imagining the red blossoms and blue skies, the road (even the potholes) carpeted with crimson needles for weeks after flowering.

Coromandel Peninsula wasn't easy to leave. Its quiet sheltered bays such as Cathedral Cove, and black sands at Hot Water Beach, and the extraordinary people living there were full of surprises. In a side valley near Coromandel, Barry Brickell indulges in both his vocation as a potter, and his hobby, a private railway. He has been working on his kilometres of small gauge railway line for about two decades. Originally he built the tracks to carry clay and timber through the dense bush hills to his pottery workshop and house. In 1986 his train engine, *Diesel Mouse*, would have occasionally pulled a load of children from the neighbourhood for a birthday ride through dense fern forest and over a ten-metre high timber bridge. Today the mini railway line, Driving Creek Railway, is a thriving summer tourist attraction, with parking for tour buses and an ice cream van.

Somewhere on the east coast south of Whitianga a roadside sign asked "Have you tasted our sweet, sweet corn?". The sign was an invitation to try "*Wilderland* organic products". We bought some plums and while they were being weighed we got talking to Dan, the 75-year-old founder of Wilderland Community, about the taste of organic food, environmental pollution, and about living. Dan works from a wheelchair ever since a serious tractor accident in the 1950s left him a paraplegic, though his disability doesn't prevent him driving around the steep land on his old converted Ferguson tractor.

Entering the property a sign declared "no drugs, no tobacco, no alcohol". This is strict policy of this community which lives in self-made timber houses scattered throughout the bushland. "Actually, when I bought these 230 hectares of land in 1964 with my wife Edith, I had no specific idea what I should do with it. The community came about incidentally more than intentionally. I had already lived in a community in the

Cathedral Cove, Coromandel Peninsula

Waikato for twenty years." Dan made a sweeping hand movement towards the dense scrubland that appeared useless for normal agriculture. "The family of three that previously owned the land couldn't live from the income that the butter and milk brought in. Today, the same land feeds thirty to forty people and supplies a shop!" His blue eyes are wide with pride.

Orchards, corn crops, avocado trees, melons and more lie hidden and sheltered amongst the scrub, in small plots. This allows the Wilderland farmers to cultivate without pesticides. Unwanted weeds are pulled out by hand. The agile Dan showed us how he weeded the gardens, sitting on an old deflated inner tube from a tractor tyre and shifting himself along between the vegetable rows. Each day a member of the community is rostered to assist Dan throughout the day. Today it was Peter, an American, who has lived at Wilderland for over eight years. We loaded up with real fruit and vegetables to last a week, and can only warn that anyone who tries Wilderland's delicious sweet corn, plums and nutty avocados will become addicted to real food. Hopefully!

Sulphur City

Rotorua 230 kilometres southeast of Auckland is the North Island's 'tourist capital'. But it stinks. "Sulphur city," as its called by the locals, lies along a thermal belt stretching from Mt Ngauruhoe to White Island in the Bay of Islands.

The Polynesian Pools shouldn't be left off the itinerary. Inconspicuous little numbers by the open air pools reveal the temperatures to be expected. While it seems only Japanese can endure the piping-hot 43 degree pool, many locals patronise the pools too. "I always come here after a long day's work outside in the rain," said John, a forestry worker. There is nothing more relaxing than lying outside under a starry night sky in a hot pool. Sharing a pool means hearing life experiences from complete strangers. An American from Los Angeles told of the latest earthquake, the forestry worker of his holiday in Bali, an Australian of her divorce.

Tapping into Rotorua's underground thermal supplies is restricted nowadays because this tourist Mecca is draining its own resources. Because nearly every hotel and motel has its own bore for private hot pools and central heating, the groundwater level has sunk and the famous Pohutu Geyser, which still reaches thirty metres in the brochures, in reality struggles to reach half that height.

Another eyecatcher in Rotorua is the bowling green in front of the old Tudor style bath-house. Lawn bowls is one of those rare team sports where neither players nor audience use colourful expletives. Here, even those with high blood pressure com-

Dan, Wilderland Community, Coromandel

ment on the game with perfect politeness: "That doesn't help at all!" or "Bad luck, friend!" Lawn bowls can be compared with either bocchia or boule. Teams play with weighted bowls on an immaculately manicured lawn that even our gentle German health shoes were not allowed to approach. Special shoes and uniforms are a matter of course. It is played by both men and women, and although traditionally played by the retired, it is attracting more and more non-retirees.

Maori have mixed feelings about Rotorua. On one hand the city is a Maori stronghold, but on the other only folklore remnants of their culture have survived. The pseudo hangi in the THC Hotel Rotorua is followed by a poi dance performance. "We have Captain Cook to thank that he discovered us," says the Maori hostess with tongue in cheek, "so we can show you our traditions in all these lovely hotels that have spread over our country." Was that Maori cynicism or an entertainer's harmless joke?

About thirty kilometres from Rotorua is the thermal park Waiotapu (sacred water) with a Champagne Pool, sixty metres in diameter and just as deep. Millions of tiny bubbles dance to the surface through the pool of hot simmering seventy degree water. Too hot and too toxic for bathing, even the edge of the natural pool is uninviting to touch. The bright-orange coloured floury substance contains not only silver and gold but mercury and arsenic. Another attraction in the park is the Lady Knox geyser. Only after she's been fed a breakfast of two kilograms of washing powder will the Lady geyser punctually rise at 10.15 a.m. Her preference for alkaline food was discovered in 1896 by accident while a group of prisoners were washing their clothes in the neighbouring pool. The powder reduces the surface tension of the underground boiling water, pressure builds and breaks the surface minutes later for the waiting cameras.

Pinus radiata

On the road south it's impossible to avoid being buffeted by the gusts of wind from the enormous logging trucks that tear along main roads between endless pine forests. Across the volcanic plateau, in the heart of the North Island, spreads the largest afforrestation area in the world. Powerful American Mack trucks loaded with enormous logs roar along the highway toward the Bay of Plenty. Tauranga (which means resting place for canoes) is New Zealand's largest export harbour, especially for kiwifruit and timber. Every year, 2.3 million tonnes of logs and 200,000 tonnes of wood chips are exported to China, Taiwan, Japan and the USA. Since more and more of the world's indigenous forests are under protection, the demand for usable timber is

Lady Knox rises daily at 10.15 a.m.

great and New Zealand can supply one per cent of the world's timber demands.

Until not so long ago *Pinus radiata* was an almost unnoticed variety of pine that grew only on the coast of California. But it is now becoming New Zealand's most profitable export. Surprisingly for a tree found in so few corners of the world, it thrives nearly everywhere in New Zealand. Indifferent to and unaffected by sandy soils, drought or frost, the Californian pine grows faster, stronger and taller than in its homeland, and with treatment after milling even attains a hardwood quality. In total approximately 1.3 million hectares have now been forested with this timber.

The pine industry is booming and many landowners have turned from traditional farming to growing *Pinus radiata*. One kilogram of high quality seeds costs more than $8,000 (about one-sixth the price of gold), but this is nonetheless an investment that promises huge profits in thirty years. A plantation of 30,000 trees planted in 1994 could bring, according to timber experts, $2 million in 2024. In 1994 over 60 million trees were planted in New Zealand.

This monoculture is controversial at times. In places like East Cape environmentalists want eroded pasture lands returned to native forest rather than forests of introduced pines. But environmentalists and the forest industry have also put their heads together to at least ensure that there will be no logging of indigenous forests in the future. Just beyond Tauranga we come to the Bay of Plenty, an area boasting another successful monoculture, the kiwifruit industry. Te Puke is New Zealand's kiwifruit capital. At the beginning of the century the seeds of the chinese gooseberry were brought to New Zealand from China and, like Pinus radiata, the fruit grew more luxuriantly here than along the Yangtze itself. Since then these green and brown "vitamin bombs" have been sold in fruit stalls all over the world.

Between May and July each year the population of Te Puke doubles. Up to ten thousand workers pick the fruit from heavily laden vines and pack them for export, all within a two-month season. In Europe the kiwifruit arrive in a perfect standardised size and egg-like shape. But at roadside stalls we could buy mis-shapen kiwifruit for as little as a dollar a kilo. "Twice as much vitamin C as an orange, twice as much vitamin E as an avocado, as much calcium as a banana, only fifty calories and heaps of fibre!" said a stall-owner convincingly. We bought three kilograms immediately – our vitamin supply for the East Cape.

East Cape

Beyond Whakatane on State Highway 35 the traffic becomes sparse. Before the 350-kilometre coastal road around East Cape

Mt. Maunganui, NZ's main timber export port

was built, this relatively infertile, hot, dry area was of little interest to European settlers. Here, in their rural stronghold, Maori have preserved their traditional lifestyles against a history in which many Maori left their homes and moved to the cities to find work. Rural maraes like those on the East Cape were abandoned. In schools children were taught in the British tradition and the Maori language was taboo. Having been robbed of their identity, many parents also became indifferent to their ancestral tongue. But for two decades Maoridom has been celebrating a revival, retrieving the self-confidence they believed was lost. In kohanga reo (language nests) children are being taught their original tongue. Run-down marae are being brought into order again and meeting houses are being strengthened and painted.

This increasing self-confidence has also created tensions in New Zealand society. Claims made on the Crown aimed at restoring justice, pride and financial security have at times been slandered as racist. "As long as the Maori remained quiet on their land, they were considered good citizens" commented a teacher about the movement. "Now that we are making careful claims, we are racists all of a sudden. That's not fair!"

In 1984 an exhibition of Maori art in New York's Metropolitan Museum of Art caused quite a stir. Art that had been suppressed, scorned, Christianised and laughed at for many hundreds of years had become socially acceptable. This acknowledgement was partly due to the effectiveness of tourism marketing, the fading of the British tradi-

tion, and the invasion of the American way of life, which caused many Pakeha to envy the rich cultural history of the native Maori. Many Pakeha today accept Maori culture as a part of their own heritage. Although crime rates amongst young Maori and Pacific Islanders are rising and a latent racism stirs, at the same time Maori language courses are being offered all over the country for

Pakeha too. Who wouldn't want to understand a little of the language with so many of the place names being of Maori origin?

In Te Kaha on East Cape where Maori has always been the local language, they managed to prevent a flood of settlers moving in. Here the Maori seem proud and not so uprooted as many in the larger cities. East Cape is still Maori country.

"Just go on over to the marae!" a jolly, plump fellow reassured us, (he wore a red checked shirt too) pointing towards the quietly standing crowd. We were drawn onto the marae by melodious Maori singing. The frightening blood red carved figure (tekoteko) with outstretched tongue and wide staring eyes above the whare runanga (meeting house) was uninviting to strangers like ourselves. "The funeral ceremony is nearly finished, then we have a feast, a hangi. Pakehas are also welcome to join us!"

The carved timber house represents the body of an ancestor. The decoration on the apex of the roof is typical for a whare or Maori meeting house. The carved tekoteko on the roof depicts Maori ancestors who arrived in canoes from Eastern Polynesia hundreds of years ago. The paddle shows both purpose and direction; the elaborately carved maihi or bargeboards represents arms; the ridge beam, the spine; and the rafters the ribs of ancestors. At the apex of the roof, above the entrance, (the head of the ancestor) a challenging almost threatening mask meets the visitor, but the tongue poked out to one side is interpreted as friendly.

Hui – a gathering, wedding, or tangihangi (the three-day funeral ceremony) – are significant affairs in Maori life. At tangi, the ritual mourning for the dead ends with a hangi, or feast. For three days the open coffin, surrounded by photographs and a case of personal belongings, remains on the verandah. Mourners gather on the marae, the area in front of the meeting house.

Traditionally the tribe's older women, or kuia, lament the dead with a karanga, a long heart-breaking wailing that calls the living and sings for the return of the spirit to its ancestral homeland in Hawaiki. The *waiata tangi,* song of mourning, is often an original composition. When the Minister announces "and now we'll sing the hymn on page twenty-three" a chorus of beautiful harmonies and soft melodies drift over the marae and across the coastal road – only the very last word reminds us of a Christian connection: Amen!

It was time for the hangi, which is the term for an earth oven. A hole about a cubic metre in size is dug, and an enormous fire lit inside it, then stones as big as footballs are thrown on top of the pyre. When the superheated stones have sunk into the glowing embers, cloth parcels of raw meat and vegetables are placed in metal cages, wrapped in wet sacking, and lowered onto the now dampened and steaming stones. All available helpers frantically shovel the earth over the cages and the food is left to cook in the ground.

About three hours later the hangi was uncovered, revealing perfectly cooked kumara (sweet potato), wild pork, beef and chicken now with an earthy smoky flavour. Our table neighbours didn't know the deceased either but they belong to the same Apanui tribe. "Tangi-hangi isn't only our three-day funeral," explains the Minister's son (Church of England), "it's simply our way of life. Nobody knew how many people might turn up today. It's not a family gathering, here our whole tribe

may come together. That's not like you Pakeha."

Three days of therapeutic, uninhibited crying eventually gave way to laughing and talking and then it was time for us to leave. The departure was warm as we hongi with our hosts. The hongi, or pressing of noses, signifies friendship "your pain is my pain," and "life goes on".

Back on the road again we could only guess what sort of traffic lay ahead. The road became slipperier as we drove, then around a curve a herd of cattle brought us to

a standstill. Drovers. Prerequisites for being a drover are good boots and patience to accompany 800 cattle on a six month drove. George and Raymond were gentle men of few words. Every day they towed their home, a caravan, with an old horse truck to the next overnight stop. Their clients were a couple of farmers outside Auckland who had bought the cattle in Gisborne at an autumn sale but didn't need them on their grazing land until spring. Droving was once an ordinary part of farming life, but since

the introduction of cattle trucks, it has become a dying profession. Cattle are moved five to six kilometres a day, grazing on the side of the road as they go. At the end of each day the drovers rest for a night though sometimes they may stop for a few days or a week. Grazing pastures are arranged in advance.

Drivers often become impatient with this harmless traffic jam and the well-fertilised tar-seal road. But droving is still permissible through an old right-of-way law. "As long as it's the Queen's Highway we're allowed on it." Although a few cattle are lost through accidents, theft or illness, droving not only allows farmers to avoid expensive trucking costs, it also protects their pastures from overgrazing, and their cattle arrive content and well-fed.

Ruatoria, 130 kilometres north of Gisborne, is the centre for Ngati Porou, the largest tribe on East Cape. From this tribe came Maoridom's most renowned Maori politician, Sir Apirana Ngata (1874-1950). He was the first Maori to attain a university degree, and represented his people as a Member of Parliament for thirty-eight years.

At Ruatoria we stayed with a man Karl met during the Waitangi Day gathering at Waitangi. John was one of those participating in the haka, the Maori war dance that was performed for Prince Charles. While all the other dancers had had their faces specially painted with moko (tattoos), John and his wife Donna wear their moko permanently.

He had answered Karl's question of whether he could photograph them both curtly, "Just one picture!" A few explanatory words were followed by a long discussion, and further photos and finally a slip of paper with John's address in a village on East Cape. Why don't we look them up?

Moko – spiral facial tattoos and body tattoos – once depicted rank, beauty and tribal affiliation, and conferred *mana* or spiritual power to the wearer. The women usually decorated themselves with special chin and lip tattoos. At the end of the last century this cultural body art had all but died out. Missionaries dismissed moko as primitive symbols. Modern tattoos replaced traditional moko and western fashions such as beards and lipstick took care of the rest. But

like other aspects of Maori culture the moko is celebrating a comeback. Young Maori, especially males, have begun to decorate their faces with the fern spirals worn by their ancestors, possibly as an expression of protest, or sign of belonging to a gang or simply a demonstration of their origins. John's facial moko exists from his time in prison. Behind bars, marks of strength and gang affiliation are popular. Instead of the traditional pigment made from burnt kauri gum and pig fat, today modern inks are applied. Of course stone chisels and steel blades have long since been replaced by electric tattoo needles. But it still remains a painful cosmetic surgery.

John and Donna are Rastafarians, seeing themselves as rebels against the governing whites, but also against the lethargy of their own tribe. Many Rastafarians have retreated to a remote corner of East Cape. Their moko binds them together, but at the same time excludes them from society. A tattooed face, to many New Zealanders, still smells of gang trouble-the prejudices are still strong.

At first we too were somewhat on edge being amongst the Rastafarians. We weren't prejudiced, rather we had been influenced by a film that we had seen a few days earlier in Auckland. *Once were Warriors*, a box-office hit in New Zealand and centre of attention at the Cannes Film Festival, had gotten under our skin. Its director, Lee Tamahori usually produces television commercials. This film, about violence (with lots of it), and the strengths and weaknesses of people and the Maori culture, was unforgettable, and the whole audience departed the cinema shattered and speechless. The story, which centres on an unemployed father and husband, who drinks, as do his mates, and beats his wife and children, is set in a Maori community in the suburbs of Auckland. The eldest son goes through the horrible initiation ceremony of a Maori gang. The film ends with hope as the main character and heroine, the mother, finally escapes the vicious circle of violence that she was trapped in, seeking support in her Maori roots, her tribe and her faith in Maori tradition. Direct and hard hitting, it had the whole nation discussing Maori and domestic issues.

Baking bread in the marae kitchen

Scenes from this film remained strongly in our minds as we drove along the dusty winding gravel road down a valley where John's mother said the Rastafarians were meeting this particular weekend. Here John and some dozen other followers had gathered at their tribal marae to discuss a possible new future. Their moko hindered their efforts to find employment and they were often driven to committing crime – a vicious circle.

We were prepared to be made unwelcome and unwanted by the group. That we, as whites armed also with cameras, wouldn't be welcomed with open arms could be historically grounded. So with a degree of apprehension we parked our campervan next to a rusting wreck near the marae. We'd hardly arrived when an excited cheerful voice cried "Haere mai! Haere mai! Please wait in front of the main entrance."

We knew it wasn't correct to go onto a marae without an invitation (an important rule to respect). John's mother had announced our coming by telephone and the group wanted to give us a traditional welcome. Tradition says that the guests of the marae should enter through the carved main entrance. Apia, a friendly lady, took us by the hand and showed us to a wooden bench and motioned us to be seated. She would guide us through the welcoming ceremony. Meanwhile two dozen wild looking figures gathered opposite us in sombre, oversized coats, twisted, matted hair, and green, yellow and red knitted caps. Nearly all of them wore moko. I thought of James Cook, a farmer's son from Yorkshire. What

was he feeling when he first stood opposite Maori faces in 1769?

John, the leader, stepped forward and began a speech: "Haere mai, haere mai." "Welcome…" said Apia whispering the translation. His speech was followed by a song. These frightening faces surprised us by singing a soft harmonious song about the future, love, peace and god. It was one of the most moving experiences we had in the Antipodes.

There was a second speaker, followed by a second song. And after the third speaker it was our turn. Oratory is a man's business. Karl humbly stuttered to express our feelings and the honour we felt to be greeted

with a ceremony steeped in such tradition. Our apprehensions had by now melted away, but we still had to give a song in return. I must be honest. Karl and I have few talents when it comes to singing. What could we possibly sing? Our lack of culture was exposed. In our desperation we came up with a Christmas carol, but soon after the first verse of "Silent Night", ran out of words. The grim-looking Maoris picked up where we stopped and we sank with shame. We, who attempt to portray other cultures, couldn't even master our own folk songs. We are better prepared now!

Beckoning us forward, a hand was stretched out and John gently pulled us

Preparing an earth oven – "hangi"

towards him and pressed his nose twice on ours. To be greeted with the hongi, the mingling of the breath of life, was an exceptional honour. It makes a handshake or even a hug seem superficial by comparison. Twelve, fifteen, twenty noses presented themselves to be pressed. Fierce dark eyes amongst details of faded and fresh tattoos moved toward our pale noses.

The ice had been broken and we were able to move freely around the marae. Apia was also a visitor. Her husband Bill, a social worker, was holding a group workshop with the young Maori gang. The topic: "How are we going to get away from crime, how can we financially support ourselves and become independent?" In the small meeting hall a white paper banner read "The future is not some place I'm going, it's something I'm creating!" For several days they hadbeen discussing this future, drawing dreams on large sheets of white paper. The words mana and papa (mother earth) were mentioned again and again. With Bill was a lawyer and an accountant brought along at the request of the gang. They were to explain to the "wild bunch" how to establish a co-operative, what a book of accounts is, and what to know when purchasing land. The gang's dream was to found a rural co-operative.

The seminar room used by the group is the dining room and adjoining kitchen next to the whare. The whare is the most sacred meeting place of a tribe. On the wall panels photos of deceased relatives documented family history. Here the roots of the tribe come together. And at the end of the day, the "body of the ancestor" offered shelter. Everyone sleeps together in the whare and mattresses, floral sheets and blankets were offered to us. To the left John and Donna snuggled their year-old twins between them. To the right, Mike, a particularly fierce-looking fellow with a dark and almost finished moko, was already snoring.

Although John had introduced us as photographers in his welcoming speech, Karl's camera remained in its bag on the first day. We didn't want to make too many demands on our first encounter. We just sat and listened as they discussed the minutiae of their lives, their dreams and beliefs, and revealed too their lack of hope. Only on the following day, after we'd sized one another up, did Karl dare to take photographs. Moko are very photogenic but they are also a very private matter to the wearer. Tattooed Maori can react fiercely to being photographed, especially without being asked. This should be respected by visitors.

On the last day of possibly a historic meeting, one that could change their lives, it was agreed they would meet again in several months. Engineers would be invited to advise them about building inexpensive housing and the optimal use of land. Whether this was all hot air or a new beginning, only the future will tell.

Part of John's bold plans are to eventually establish an autonomous Maori region on

Donna with her twins, East Cape

East Cape. A fanciful utopian dream it may seem, but it's one that has been pursued in this area before, most famously by Te Kooti, a charismatic Maori warrior who escaped from prison in 1868 and hid for twenty years amongst the forests of the Urewera, leading a bloody rebellion against colonial settlers.

Te Kooti was offered protection by the Tuhoe people, the "Children of the Mist" whose home in the Huiarau Range lies today in Te Urewera National Park, our next destination. At 210,000 hectares, the park is the largest expanse of primeval forest in the North Island. The region is one of the most impenetrable in the North and is accessible by State Highway 38, a snaking gravel road. While the South Island enjoys a reputation for its great wildness, a big adventure is certainly to be had driving inland from the East Cape. Both State Highway 38 and even the Gentle Annie Road are *the* overland roads in New Zealand.

Over six hours we met three cars, a racing Bedford school bus and a herd of wild horses led by a ghostly white stallion. But there were no petrol stations. Tight blind corners, unprotected precipices, and occasional falling stones required full concentration. To enjoy the podocarp forest and kauri giants one must continually stop to peer up into the mist.

Somewhere along the road in a grassy river valley we came across two house trucks parked in an idyllic camp. White smoke spiralling from an open fire diffused into the valley, and washing hung from a long rope. House trucks are the ultimate

Kiwi statement of independence and do-it-yourself mentality. Old school buses and Bedford trucks provide the foundation, the rest comes from imagination, paint and treasures from junk heaps and demolition yards.

Mark has lived for twenty-six years in house trucks, and this was his third Ford. His wife Kiri belongs to the Tuhoe tribe, a genuine child of the mist, although she and Mark are rarely here in Urewera. Instead they wander wherever they wish in New Zealand, working on building sites or in

freezing works, then retreating again for months to the bush.

Their home was a fantasy in wood, every detail lovingly handcrafted. Daylight fell through stained-glass windows, a cast-iron stove provides warmth, and a timber fender protected the children from the fire. Solar cells provide enough electricity for lights and a television. Even the kitchen corner with sink and gas stove was a masterpiece. A cavity underneath the floor served as cold storage, and a ladder led up to roomy sleeping quarters.

The heyday of mobile castles like these lies in the past. Stricter laws have made the survival of old trucks difficult, and many are now hidden behind farm houses or in gardens of outer suburbs. The trend today in housetrucking is more towards converting roadworthy former school buses.

It rained in sheets as we approached the heart of the park by Lake Waikaremoana. But without rain, no rainforest, without mist, no children of the mist. We parked our standard reliable but unromantic campervan near the lake and began our routine kitchen duty. That evening leftovers were on the menu: delicacies from the hangi given to us by the Rastafarians as a farewell gift. We served up chicken, kumara, potatoes and broccoli, and opened a bottle of Te Mata Cabernet, ideal for a rainy evening in the Urewera.

The next morning exceeded all our expectations. Below on the lake, thick white fog was already being burned off by the sun. Armed with Goretex and gloves we searched for a way heavenwards and found Waitiri Point and a viewing platform. Slowly the mist dissipated, and when the wind tried to blow holes in the fog we glimpsed the lake. Yes, that must be the home of the Children of the Mist.

Te Urewera National Park offers tramping over several days, and short day trips, like the one to Lake Waikareiti, a mountain lake at 300 metres. A few minutes away from the main road we were enveloped by the quietness and shadows of a rain forest. We clambered over giant fallen trees clad in moss and brushed against the curled fronds of new fern growth. It was mid May, late autumn, and deciduous fuchsia trees already had yellowed leaves. In just two hours, without having seen a soul, we reached the lake where the water was so still the forest edge was reflected on the surface. A couple of row boats waited on the sandy beach for fishermen, water lapped the aluminium hulls. It was quiet, so quiet.

Ring of Fire

Barely eighty kilometres as the crow flies west of here is Lake Taupo, a day's drive by car. Lake Taupo is, according to Maori legend, the pulsating heart of the mythical fish caught by "Maui" that formed the body of the North Island. It's hard to believe that this area was the stage for one of the largest and most devastating volcanic eruptions in the last million years, even greater than the eruption of Krakatoa in Indonesia in 1863, and thirty times more violent than the Mt St Helens eruption in 1980. The eruption took place in 186 AD long before the Maori set foot on the island. How is it possible to know this without any local documentation? There were chroniclers, not in New Zealand, but in China and in Rome. By radiocarbon dating, experts are able to tell approximately when mountains were active. In 186 AD a Chinese historian at the Emperor's palace described a phenomenon where the sun rose in the east blood red, and only became bright when it was high in the sky. Also, from a Roman source

(Scriptores Historiae Augustae) it is understood that in the same autumn the sky had glowed strangely.

Long ago says Maori legend, when the mountains lived and loved, the beautiful green bush clad Pihanga (north of Mt Tongariro) attracted suitors from the mountain world. All of them wanted her as a wife, but she loved only Tongariro, and the others left defeated. These must have been fiery passionate times.

Later in mythical times, after the ancestors of Maori arrived, Ngatoro-i-rangi (chief of the legendary Te Arawa canoe) lit a fire on the peak of Tongariro as a sign claiming land for his people. At the gods' wishes, he ordered his followers to wait and fast until his return. He climbed the mountain with his slave Ngauruhoe. Below, his companions could wait no longer, they had to eat. This angered the gods and they sent hailstorms and fierce icy winds. Their chief nearly perished. To temper the gods' anger he sacrificed his slave Ngauruhoe. The gods answered and sent fire underground to rescue the frozen newcomers. Today Ngauruhoe together with Ruapehu (exploding fire) and Tongariro (on the south wind) form the three volcanic cones of Tongariro National Park.

This is New Zealand's oldest national park. A visionary Maori chief gave the volcanic area to the government in 1887 on the condition that his ancestors' burial grounds remain a protected area. He knew even then that this was the only way he could possibly save this place of gods and myths from the greed of white men.

Unesco further acknowledged the park's significance in 1990 by declaring it a World Heritage Area. Geologically the park is in the middle of an active volcanic zone that stretches from Mt Taranaki on the west coast through Rotorua and on to White Island in the Bay of Plenty. This zone is part of the Pacific Ring of Fire, a chain of active vulcanism on the edge of the Pacific crustal plate. When the gods will again be angry is a relevant question in this area. When we set off to walk the Tongariro Crossing the seismograph in the park's headquarters lay sleeping in a corner. But in 1996 the eruption of Ruapehu was seen in all its glorious power on television screens all over the globe.

Mt Tongariro's moon-like volcanic landscape, with its snowcapped peaks, hot pools and emerald coloured lakes is one of the most popular tramping areas in the South Pacific. Its four mountain huts have to cope with 5,000 overnights and 12,000 day-hikers each year. The mountain gods seemed somewhat restless when we departed Whakapapa village. After about an hour we reached the open tussock plains under the northern slope of Ruapehu, the North Island's highest mountain at 2,797 metres. Hardly out of the shelter of stunted beech forest we were blasted by an icy southerly wind that brought hail and bad tempers. South in the Southern Hemisphere means cold. And a southerly, even in high summer, is unrelenting. "Be prepared for sunburn and snowstorms," a friend in Auckland warned us "and both on the same day!"

→ 157

Mount Cook or Aoraki - the "cloud piercer"

The massive glaciers
of the Southern Alps

Mt Tasman, Mt Cook and the Southern Alps

Twilight at Mueller Hut, Mount Cook National Park

Last Light on Mount Cook

The reflection on lake Matheson is perfect, the photograph is upside down

Kahikatea trees thrive on swampy ground, Lake Wahapo

Black sands near
Okarito, West Coast

Okarito's beach and lagoon seen from Trig Point

33

Black metallic sand promises gold, West Coast

A few ounces of gold dust

Gold prospectors, John and Mark

Home at Gillespies Beach

A cup of tea for the visitors

Greg and his dairy cows, West Coast Road

Sheepdogs after a long day's work

School outing to Paparoa National Park

Punakaiki or Pancake Rocks at Dolomite Point

Ice cathedrals of Franz Josef glacier in Westland

Waterfalls everywhere...

... even from the moss...

thick soft carpets..

.. or even just a thin skin

Gillespies Beach and Otorokua Point, West Coast

River mouth of the Cook River at the Tasman Sea

Sutherland Falls and Lake Quill, Fiordland

Doubtful Sound, where the Tasman Sea reaches 20 kms inland

45

View from Wilmot Pass
over Doubtful Sound

46

Ice, wind and water formed the sounds of Fiordland

Dick lifts the bounty
after two hours flying

Jeff's sharp eyes search for deer in the tussock of Fiordland

Jeff packs the net into its case

A wild and dangerous hunt

Both hunters work like birds of prey

1.2 million hectares of
wilderness : Fiordland

Silver beech forest along the Routeburn River, Mt Aspiring National Park

In the kingdom of fairies and elves

A fairytale world of mosses and lichens, Routeburn Track

Walking the Caples Track

The trail follows the Caple River to its mouth

Mouth of the Arthur River in Mitford Sound

Autumn muster of
14,000 sheep in the
Carvie Mountains

58

Getting ready for dinner

Dinner in Jack Mack's Hut

Good cards or a bluff Skip?

Thick fog outside, waiting for better weather, Jack Mack's Hut

The first snow-fall overnight, Garvie Mountains

Even here it's getting uncomfortable

Highway 8 through the tussock hills, Lindis Pass, Otago

Lakeside drive, Lake Wakatipu near Queenstown

View across to the
Remarkable Mountains

Idyllic views even from this secluded spot

Autumn frost, Mackenzie Country, Otago

Arthur's Pass connects the east and west coast

With the budgie on holiday, Lake Tekapo

Kea prefer windscreen wiper rubbers, Homer Tunnel

Half a million sheep at minus 18°C, Mataura Freezer Works

Fred and Myrtle in their Paua house, Bluff.

Oamaru's deserted main street on a Sunday

Cathedral Square in the centre of "British" Christchurch.

The dining hall
at Christ's College

Lunchtime for students at Christ's College

Rex, farmer with his
dogs, Banks Peninsula

Lyttelton Harbour, Banks Peninsula near Christchurch

Old Lighthouse at Nugget Point, Catlins

Podocarp forest along the Tahakopa River, Catlins

Few forests survived the axe in the Catlins

Nature's marbles, Moeraki Boulders, east coast

Whale-watching along the east coast near Kaikoura

With some luck a school of dolphins may appear

No thoroughfare - a barrier of Drysdale rams, Flax Hills

Shearing competition, Whangarei

Shearer's meal, Tarawera

Sweeping sands, Mutton Cove, Abel Tasman National Park

"Take nothing but photos – leave nothing but footprints"

Abel Tasman National Park, with backpack..

... or with sea kayaks to isolated coves

A labyrinth of land and water, Marlborough Sounds

Wellington the
"Windy City"

93

Government House . second largest timber building in the world

Old St. Paul's
in Wellington

95

Roofscape of Athfield's house above Wellington Harbour

Victorian timber houses at Oriental Bay, Wellington

Still life with "paua" or abalone shells, Cape Palliser

A rare catch for Charlie, Okavita

Lawn bowls - a popular sport for the older generation

"Full up" in the Puhoi Hotel

Te Mata Winery, near Havelock North

Ben and his praying mantis, Hastings

Sea of fog above
Tukituki Valley

Views from Te Mata Peak, Havelock North

Literally – "moving house", near Palmerston North

Leon with his son, house-truck nomads, Urewera

Champagne Pool, a 900-years-old crater lake, Waiotapu

Pohutu Geyser, Whakarewarewa

Thermal power
Station, Wairakei

Golden Fleece Terraces at Orakeikorako

Coromandel, a couple of hours from Auckland

Moon crescent above
Coromandel Harbour

Cathedral Cove, eroded by wind and water, Coromandel

114

More than 160 varieties of fern can be found in New Zealand

F. Hundertwasser's bottle house

Designing a new kiwi flag

In front of his house, Bay of Islands

Barry's bath room

Driving Creek Railway, Coromandel

The potter Barry Brickell

Dan, aged 75 (in wheelchair) founded Wilderland Community 30 years ago

Musical family, Wildeland, Coromandel

"It was warmer earlier folks!" - Shearing shed, Taihape

Wool Stores in Napier

Ruapehu's crater lake never freezes, Tongariro National Park

View above Blue Lake, Mt Ngauruhoe and Mt Ruapehu

Tussock grass in the Rangipo Desert, Tongariro

Red Crater, Tongariro National Park

Ketetahi Hut, above
Lake Rotoaira

Blue lake on the plateau of Mt Tongarir

Weekly sheep auction in Hamilton, Waikato

Farmers near
Reporua, East Cape

A typical "bach" or holiday house, East Cape

George and Ray in their caravan

For decades they've worked as drovers

It's a dying profession

800 cattle and 6 months on the road

A "Kuia", a woman elder at a funeral in Tekaha, East Cape

Funeral ceremony, marae, Te Kaha

Hongi, welcome greeting

Food cooked in the earth oven, hangi

Hangi, the funeral banquet

Maori ceremony, "haka" for the Prince of Wales, Waitangi

John and Donna question the Treaty of Waitangi

Moko or traditional facial tatoos have long since died out

Maori rastafarians plan a new future, East Cape

John, leader of the group with his daughter

Gannet colony at Muriwai, West coast near Auckland

Gannets rarely nest on the mainland.

Piha, a popular surfing beach on the North Island

Surf fishing on Auckland's west coast

Auckland is home to more than a quarter of New Zealand's population

Ponsonby, Auckland's colourful city suburb

Auckland, New Zealand's secret capital and "City of Sails"

Fishing by Auckland's Harbour Bridge

Yearling auction at Karaka, bids of up to a million dollars

Female jockeys ready to race at Auckland race course

Anzac Day in Kaitaia; a war veteran shows his medals

Sunday service for Polynesians in Auckland

Timber Ratana church at Te Kao, Northland

Kerewai explains
flax weaving to us

Sand dunes near Te Paki, Northland

View over Werahi Beach and Cape Maria van Diemen

Cape Reinga Lighthouse, New Zealand's northernmost point

Tongariro

Two Germans dressed for an Antarctic expedition, packed in Goretex suits, woollen hats, gloves and sunglasses approached us with frozen red noses. They carried bad news. "The wind was so vicious we had to crawl on our hands and knees to get around the crater ridge!" Meanwhile we too were snug in our gloves and "polyprops." Long polypropolene leggings worn under shorts is standard "made in New Zealand" tramping clothing. They don't impede leg movement, are excellent protection against cold, and they dry within minutes after rain showers. But would they be adequate for the Tongariro Crossing?

Shortly before sunset we arrived at Mangetepopo hut wearing every piece of clothing we had, having started out eating ice cream and wearing not much more than sunblock. A universal "Hi!" is said by all in the hut. "In the corner are a couple of vacant mattresses!" called someone responding to our concerned faces. It was very busy in this twenty-five bed hut, which is on one of the most popular of New Zealand's "Great Walks" tramping network. Dinner time. Japanese, Americans, a few Irish and a couple of Australians (surprisingly few Germans) dug supplies out of their backpacks and prepared fast food in aluminium pots. Karl had it easy – his meal comes out of a freeze-dried vacuum-packed astronaut's dinner packet enticingly labelled "curried beef and green beans", to which he added heaps of basmati rice and garlic.

Looking for light switches was a waste of time, but the hut was fitted out with toilets, water tanks and gas burners. A few candles threw enough light for a Japanese to darn socks, and the Irish to play "500", while at the American table traveller's tales were exchanged. The news of the day: two young women from Boston, despite the storms and freezing temperatures, ventured to the 2,291 metre summit of Ngauruhoe and "saw nothing but our shadowy selves and a few rocks."

It was a restless night. The angry gods of Tongariro sent stormy messengers, thrashing out their rage on the iron roof and under the eaves. In the morning the Irish contingent were first to peel themselves out of their sleeping bags and light the wood stove. Soon the smell of toast, hissing gas, bubbling pots of porridge and the aroma of instant coffee (the only time it has an aroma) wafted through the hut. On the rough wooden tables, competing muesli mixtures and breads were spread out for attention.

Around ten, the blue-black clouds were lit by sunlight and everyone pored over their 1:80,000 maps to plan their routes. Kerry, the warden, received the latest weather report by radio (run on a solar battery) and announced "It's looking better! Clouds should be clearing and winds are dying down and temperatures rising." As people packed she reminded us not to forget to fill in the intentions book before hitting the track. "We want to know your whereabouts in case your mothers give us a call." She smiles, but means it seriously.

Wooden poles marked the way between blocks of lava. At Soda Springs the track climbs steeply for 250 metres to Mangatepopo Saddle. The clouds had been swept away by the good spirits and now only factor 20 sunblock, sunglasses and a hat helped against the easily underestimated intensity of the sun.

On the saddle we couldn't decide whether to go upwards or onwards. "Three hours for the return trip" to Ngauruhoe's summit advised the Department of Conservation (DOC) leaflet. The 2,500-year-young volcano was immaculate, its grey symmetrical scoria slopes sweeping up to 2,291 metres into the now steely blue sky. We left our backpacks behind a lava boulder in the shade and out of sight. We had to go up.

There was no path up the mountain, rather it was a free for all. Two metres up and oops! a metre back down. It was like climbing a vertical wall of loose gravel; with the sun beating down on our backs and there was a glaring reflection from the grey rocks in front. For most it was an easy climb but I sank into the stones and the stones sank into my boots, a most uncomfortable feeling at first. I took two arduous hours to zigzag to the top.

However, it was exhilarating reaching the crater rim and being blasted by an icy biting wind. Without gloves and woollen hats it would have been unbearable. It smelt like hell as sulphur fumes spiralled from cracks in the lava rocks. Overnight, the earth's breath had frozen to form five-centimetre long fingers of ice.

From the summit breathtaking views in all directions was the reward for the uphill struggle. In the distant west was Mt Taranaki, behind us was the highest North Island volcano, Mt Ruapehu. Opposite was Tongariro, the smallest of the volcano gods. To the north, Red Crater lay like an open wound and beyond that Lake Rotoaira and Lake Taupo. We wandered around the crater's edge with the Americans. John, a Kiwi from the Bay of Islands, had found a sheltered corner in the sun and was listening to rock classics from his "walkman".

The descent was much easier. Using your heels and imagination it was like running down a sand dune. Those with know-how and spare socks lunge down in 10 minutes. Going faster is helped by recalling the warning notices in the motorcamp: "what to do in the event of an eruption". It was in 1976 when this Ngauruhoe last spat out ash. With these thoughts I shortened my descent time by about ten minutes.

Although this national park is often described as a moonscape, it is anything but monotone. The tramp through this 2.5-million-year-old landscape must be one of the most colourful in New Zealand. Continuing on our way we followed the poled route through the flat dry south crater to where it rises to 1,886 metres at Red Crater. Inside, black, red and yellow powdery colours seem to have been drawn from the devil's palette. The path descends a narrow ridge to the stunning milky-green Emerald Lakes set like jewels in a red-brown and black cloak.

The sun crawled towards the horizon and once again we were the stragglers on the track. While other trampers were soaking their freeze-dry meals at the huts, we enjoyed the best light of the day above the tempting but icy waters of Blue Lake. Ketetahi hut lies on the north flank of Tongariro, above the treeline amongst a sea of tussock grass. The hut kept us inside long enough to cook fish in tomato sauce padded out with red lentils. Far below our weary feet lay Lake Rotoaira, and beyond that Lake Taupo shimmered in the last light of day. The moon rose behind Pihanga, the much fought over, bush-clad loved one of Tongariro.

A soak in the hot springs at Ketetahi had to wait until the next day. The springs are on the downhill path to the main road and exit. But be warned this isn't a thermal park like Rotorua with fences and paths to keep to. Hot steaming clouds and several warning signs told of the dangers to nonchalant strangers. Here the earth's crust can be hot and thin. Miniature geysers shoot up in one-minute tempo from rock fissures, and sulphurous boiling mud pools reveal a devil's playground.

Just above this thermal chaos a path led over a ridge into a small enclave where rocks have been used to dam small steam-

The crater rim of Mt Ngauruhoe

ing pools. We found four terraced pools and tested the temperature carefully first before climbing in. In the first and highest pool, no bigger than three bath tubs, the water was boiling hot, only for soup cubes. The second was for experienced Japanese. The third, twenty metres down the slope, was just right. But be warned, not only is the water hot in this bath tub, so is the surrounding ground.

Ketetahi means food basket, and the Maori used the boiling waters for cooking. In effect we're bathing in their kitchen. Hot pools were also revered by settlers at the beginning of the century for their healing properties for rheumatic conditions. When we set off that morning we knew we'd miss the shuttle bus that collects trampers from the car park below Okahukura Bush at ten every morning. But to hell with civilisation!

The next day we aimed to reach Mt Taranaki. In good weather the classic volcanic cone towers above the horizon and can be seem from great distances. But we were to be disappointed again. We've made five attempts to see Mt Egmont, as many Pakeha still call it, at close quarters, but each time it's grandeur has been hidden under a cloudy blanket.

The area south of Hamilton towards Taranaki province and the Whanganui River is known as King Country. Many desperate battles took place here between Maori and the more powerful colonial armies. There are few reminders of the dense forests and marshes where the "Hau-Hau" rebels once hid. Today well-cultivated market gardens, sheep and dairy farms and horse studs dominate the landscape, allowing history to be easily forgotten.

An unsealed road from Raetihi winds through scenic, isolated, though not desolate country. From Pipiriki the gravel road follows the tranquil Whanganui River. Many of its small riverside settlements were founded as missionary posts and have illustrious names such as Atene (Athens), Koriniti (Corinth) or Ranana (London). Hiruharama (Jerusalem) lies on a picturesque river bend, overlooked by a timber church built in 1884 for a Catholic nursing order. A detour to the church is certainly worthwhile. The nave is watched over by two wall figures that cast threatening rather than devoted looks towards the statue of Jesus.

The Whanganui is New Zealand's longest navigable river. Until the middle of this century steamboats connected Wanganui on the east coast with the inland town of Pipiriki. This once flourishing tourist village was the last stop on a three-day river cruise. Only a few postcards remain as mementos of the elegant turn-of-the-century hotel that burnt down some decades ago.

Wellington

It was pouring with rain so we drove southwards to the southern point of the North Island. When we reached Wellington storm gusts shook our van – the "world's windiest city" lived up to its name. No matter if it's a cold southerly or a warm northerly, sea winds are squeezed through the wind tunnel that is Cook Strait and Wellington suffers. Aucklanders joke that you can tell a Wellingtonian away from home because he always holds on to his hat even when it's calm.

Not only are strong winds and rain ordinary occurrences in this city, so too are earthquakes. Wellington has been built on the fault line between two of the earth's continental plates – the Indo-Australian and Pacific plates. The Indo-Australian plate is gradually forcing the Pacific Plate into the earth at a rate of five centimetres a year. Not very much, but in the stratum below, enormous pressure builds up which is relieved by regular quakes and tremors, about a dozen each year. In 1931 Napier, in Hawkes Bay, was devastated by a powerful quake. Another large earthquake is overdue, the big one is awaited.

When Karl first visited Wellington in 1984 he was disappointed with the inner city's modern glassed high-rise architecture. But while working for several months with New Zealand architect, Ian Athfield, he came to know and love the city and its labyrinth of roads, the jumble of Victorian timber houses, the lifestyle of the residents, the wind, and the thousand-and-one moods of Cook Strait.

It is difficult to categorise Athfield's residence as a "house". Perched high on a steep northerly slope above a motorway, it resembles more a sculpture; inside is a maze of stairs and cave-like rooms overgrown with creepers, lit by bay windows and skylights, with no clear divisions between working and living spaces.

The Athfields began building their house and office over thirty years ago, a structure that continues to grow and creep down the hill. The massive solid-concrete appearance of the architecture is deceptive and the inspiration and execution of the design is typically Kiwi. For instance its funnel-like tower, where interior designer Clare Athfield has her studio, is nothing more than chicken wire wrapped around a timber frame covered in a cement mortar with a weatherproof coating.

The waves of settlers that came from England and Scotland in the first half of the nineteenth century had spent up to nine months in the hull of a swaying ship to escape the tenements of industrial Britain. Once here their number-one priority was to build a roof over their heads as quickly and cheaply as possible. The gold diggers brought corrugated iron over from Australia as cheap building material. "Shoe box" houses, each with four tiny rooms, a verandah (which were at first wrongly built to face south) and steep gable roof (for snow that never came), were typical of early Wellington residences. Later, as needs grew and money allowed, extensions would be added.

New Zealanders are fanatical do-it-yourself-people, and "a home of my own" is almost a number-one life priority. The thought of a rented apartment in a block of flats is for many a bad dream. Many small old homes are still in use, and in coastal or hinterland areas, often serve as a weekend holiday retreat, or bach. The term bach was probably borrowed from bachelor, and encapsulates the free independent man in his simple refuge close to the great outdoors. Today, if New Zealand's suburban roads appear deserted on weekends and on holidays, its probably because many city dwellers have retreated to the far corners of the country to stay in their baches.

Well known bach settlements are sometimes occupied all year round, like those at Birdlings Flat and Taylor's Mistake on Banks Peninsula, or the fishermen's huts at the mouth of the Rakaia River. Lines of little boxes, disused tram cars or remains of pioneer huts huddle alongside the most popular outdoor spots in the country.

The goldrush of 1860 brought architects versed in European styles to this side of the world. The results were an amalgamation of architectural design, from orderly Greek pillars to romantic fantasies in wood complete with orioles, gables and towers.

Considered an earthquake risk, many timber homes in downtown Wellington were demolished and replaced with high-rise office buildings. Wellington's former Government Buildings on Lambton Quay, built in 1876 from rimu and Tasmanian hardwoods (the world's second largest timber building after the Japanese Todaiji Temple), was also threatened with demolition but has recently been restored. Even the future of New Zealand's imposing

A Trip to Oriental Bay, Wellington

140-year-old timber church, Old St Paul's, was uncertain until 1996. Timber as a building material was apparently considered "second-rate" by the contemporary developer and Anglican missionary Bishop Selwyn. But because a more expensive stone cathedral couldn't be financed, the architect and priest Frederick Thatcher designed a wooden church anyway. Both architect and craftsmen made a virtue out of necessity, cleverly interpreting English Gothic in timber. In 1909 the church was to make way for a new cathedral, but the bishop then in office rejected the demolition orders. In 1932 it narrowly escaped demolition again, officials having decided that just a few rimu and totara beams would be included in a new concrete cathedral. The actions of a civic group and official recognition as a protected historical building, finally prevented the destruction of the church. Today it primarily serves as a concert hall and favoured place for wedding ceremonies.

Tourists from abroad are often surprised at the sprawl of unimaginative box-like architecture in New Zealand's suburbs and small towns. The depression at the beginning of the century brought architectural playfulness to an end and little money was available for decoration. Roofs became almost flat, just enough to drain rainwater. But in the late 1960s young architects like Ian Athfield and Roger Walker inspired a movement away from the shoe box architecture, instigating a rebellion against unimaginative city architecture, and against the random borrowing of international styles. Fantasy was possible even in New Zealand: citadels appeared in an ocean of box architecture, often in loud shrill colours or rough timber fronts with a mixture of elements from Victorian colonial style, pop art and the aesthetic functionalism of the farmhouse and lichen-covered shearing sheds that dominate New Zealand's landscape. The architectural details were rough, not of European refinement and therefore unspoilt. The materials: light timber frames, usually timber facings, concrete bricks or plaster – ideal for this do-it-yourself nation. Plastic, agricultural piping served as drainpipes, and corrugated iron, used since the goldrush, remains classic roofing material.

One of the most convincing architectural statements in recent years was the Wellington Public Library. New Zealand is a country of avid bookreaders, so it isn't surprising to find one of its most remarkable public libraries in the middle of the city. No musty lending library smells will be found here under the steely nikau palms on Civic Square. The open reading halls, the café, the children's corner, the book shop and the foyer are much more than a place to thumb pages. It's become a meeting point in the city centre.

Architects Ian and Clare Athfield, Wellington

South Island

I still recall my first crossing to the South Island. We were on the six o'clock evening ferry from Wellington heading across Cook Strait as the last rays of sun tinted the fiord-like landscape of the Marlborough Sounds with an almost mystical play of light and shade.

The Marlborough Sounds are a labyrinth of bays, inlets, islands and peninsulas. A flight over the mosaic of water and land is a stunning experience. Captain Cook gave his name to Cook Strait but at the same time only just avoided wrecking the *Endeavour* on rocks known as The Brothers after a sudden tide change. Today a lighthouse warns sea vessels away.

It poured with rain when we arrived in Picton. This was not usual. The northern part of the South Island boasts New Zealand's best weather, and with over 2,400 hours of sun and only 125 rainy days a year, Nelson and Marlborough are leading wine and fruit growing regions, attracting too numerous painters, potters, weavers and sun-hungry tourists. Nelson is proud of its claim to have established New Zealand's first streetside café, Chez Eelco.

Nelson city, (named after the admiral Lord Nelson), the second New Zealand Company settlement after Wellington, almost became the nation's capital. Queen Victoria enthusiastically proclaimed the small harbour town a "city" in 1858, although in those days the population was barely more than 2,500. Today 47,000 residents enjoy the "sunshine capital". In the windows of real estate offices, rotating stands offered house sales like rotisserie chickens. With $200,000 or more you could purchase a small house on the coast, but for most this is the stuff of dreams.

Barely seventy kilometres from Nelson the Abel Tasman National Park lures trampers. In 1985 a German guidebook described the park as a "hot tip". Today in summer New Zealand's smallest national

park is over-run. Admittedly, the coast track, which can be walked in jogging shoes or sometimes in sandals, is not physically demanding, and therefore, in summer at least, is not for those seeking rugged wilderness and isolation. A quick glance at the 1:50,000 map explains the reason for its popularity. The variety of ferny vegetation, sandy beaches, quiet sheltered bays and tidal flats seem like paradise, and by European standards is still relatively deserted.

The first obstacle to get past when starting the coast track from Marahau is a raspberry milkshake from the Park Café. Having filled in the obligatory intentions book and purchased hut permits we shouldered light (twelve kilogram) packs and began the fifty kilometre walk in perfect conditions, carrying sleeping bags, four days' food, wet weather gear, swimming gear, hats, sunglasses and sunblock. In case the huts were overcrowded we carried a two-man tent. Being February beds couldn't be guaranteed. (We recommend April and May as better months.) The most important thing to have here and on other tracks is insect repellent. The infamous sandflies are horrible little devils, their bite irritates and can itch for several days. Repellents can be purchased everywhere but we preferred the local potion, Tui, made of olive oil and citronella, which was more effective and less toxic than the alternatives. I also carried my trusty pink, gluggy calamine lotion which I've been using since I was a child to relieve itchy irritations.

A steady climb brought views through the bush to the ocean below. The air smelt of gum and peppery manuka, and the ferns were most spectacular! There are about 160 varieties of fern. Mamaku, the largest of the tree ferns (it grows up to twenty metres), lined the beaches, throwing beautiful filigree shadows along the way. The contrast between cool shady paths and open golden beaches is the beauty of the walk. A shadeless summer beach looks good in travel brochures, but sweaty backs and feet are bearable as long as many quick dips are made along the way.

When we arrived that evening at Anchorage hut, after several plunge stops, the hut was overflowing. "First come, first served!" There are five huts along the coast track no more than three hours walk apart. We camped outside, sleeping under just our tent lining and a starry sky. The constellations appeared upside down to European eyes – in Hanover, our home town, the night sky is no more than a dusty twenty-watt bulb compared to this.

Thirty-five kilometres (about twelve hours' walk) lay between us and Whariwharangi hut in Golden Bay. We allowed plenty of time and waited until midday for the tide to drop low enough to take the shortcut across the tidal lagoon to Torrent Bay. Rubber sandals came into their own crossing the lagoon. Slimy sinking sand and shallow pools would have otherwise meant wet boots, though going barefoot isn't advisable either because you're not alone on the tidal flats which are shared with mud crabs, razor sharp shells and worms. The flats are alive!

We followed a merry bunch of German globetrotters and a young family. "Moni, can you bring me the nappies please!" The family were conquering New Zealand's walking tracks as a trio and Jonas was part of the luggage. His mother Moni carried him in a special backpack along with the nappies (used and unused – carry out what you carry in). Mike carried the provisions and tent, a burden of twenty kilos.

Some of the best scenery, bays, fern forests and beaches lie between Bark Bay and Awaroa. Tips? Mosquito Bay and Sand-fly Bay. The names may not sound inviting, but don't be put off. Bark Bay was given its name because here bark was stripped from rimu and beech trees for use in tanning hides. Granite blocks are reminders that rocks were taken from Tonga Quarry to provide stone for the steps below Nelson Cathedral and government buildings in Wellington.

Awaroa Bay is one of the highlights of the hike. For decades its sweeping beaches, huge banks of shells and a wide estuary have attracted both walkers and boaties.

More or less well-concealed holiday homes and a lodge have been built into the park's bush. A wooden sign painted with welcoming sunflowers pointed us towards the Awaroa Café. To find ourselves sitting in its massive artistic wooden chairs, drinking freshly squeezed orange juice, was an unexpected surprise. We spent our dollars on a tempting organic salad and plum cake and cream.

For two hours before and after low tide it is possible to wade across Awaroa estuary by foot. From here the way is nearly all along beaches. In a broad sweep the coastline brought us to Totaranui which for many is the last stop along the track. But don't give up here! Without doubt the most dramatic part of the track, certainly the highest and most isolated stretch, is the section between Totaranui and Wainui Inlet.

From Totaranui to Whariwharangi, the northernmost hut, is only a three-and-a-half hour hike. The northerly Anapai Bay and Mutton Cove are exposed to strong ocean currents and few sea kayaks dare come this distance. It was somewhere near here in Golden Bay that Abel Tasman attempted to make the first recorded European landing in New Zealand.

Abel Tasman had been sent to this part of the world in 1642 by the Dutch East India Company to search for the great southern continent *Terra australis incognita*. On December 13 his fleet was confronted by the west coast of the South Island, a "land uplifted high". They went northwards and eventually anchored in what is now called Golden Bay. Smoke on shore signalled signs of life. But before the Dutch could set foot on the land there was a skirmish with the Maori, who had approached in their war canoes, and Tasman lost four men (from today's viewpoint each party to the skirmish must have seemed wholly alien to one another). He gave the bay the profound name of Murderers Bay and hurriedly set sail. He never did land anywhere else on these newly found islands.

We reached Whariwharangi hut on the western edge of the park next to a beach without footprints. This place is a small piece of paradise, the hut there being a converted two-storey farmhouse with a cosy kitchen, spacious bunkrooms and a welcoming verandah sheltered by huge macrocarpa trees.

It's also opossum country, and at twilight possums came raining out of the trees to scavenge food, cheekily trying to get scraps from tired table guests. These cute (to us) furry creatures were introduced to New Zealand from Australia in 1837 in an effort to introduce a fur trade. Instead, possums have become a dangerous threat to New Zealand's native plants and birds. Seventy million of these hungry creatures consume not only bird's eggs, but enormous quantities of foliage, systematically destroying native forest. A solution is not yet in sight!

The evening meal at Whariwharangi turned into a gourmet extravaganza. Marcel, one of our German tramping companions, harvested green-lipped mussels off the rocks, a huge blackened pot was set on the camp fire, and we were invited to join in a farewell dinner as we were all going separate ways the next day. Karl and I left early in the morning to catch the water taxi back to Kaiteriteri and civilisation.

Of dogs and whales

On our first visit to New Zealand in 1986 we had prepared an exact schedule involving ten weeks for the South Island and six weeks for the North. We had naively planned only two days for the east coast drive down to Christchurch. Then, on a short detour to Hanmer Springs, a flat tyre on the second day threw our plans in the air. It was supposed to be a little detour to Hanmer Springs. The ten minute tyre change led to an invitation for a cup of tea in a nearby farmhouse, and from there we were directed to a local sheep dog trial and we stayed four days. I hid the schedule somewhere in the back of the car…

"The dog trial is over at the neighbour's place," Judy explained before we hurtled down a dusty fifteen kilometre road in her pickup truck. A sticker on her vehicle "Real men don't wear polyester!" advertised that Judy and Bill raise sheep.

Halfway up a hill about twenty utility vehicles and conventional cars were parked next to a corrugated iron shed. A generator roared away behind the shed ensuring that a fridge kept ice cream and beer cold. Mothers sold home-made apple pies and red, tasteless sausages on sticks: saveloys. Profits went to the local primary school.

Without dogs farmers would be helpless against the millions of merinos, romneys, perendales and halfbreds on New Zealand sheep farms. Training sheep dogs is a skill

Motorized team, Morven Hills station

and dog trials, a New Zealand invention, offers farmers a chance to display their abilities. The first trial apparently took place in 1867 in Otago. Today the national championships are an important sporting event, and are broadcast on television.

"Get in behind Paaaauuul!" yelled Bill desperately. One long whistle proved effective. Paul, a black and white Kelpie-Collie mix, circled around three sheep and forced them discreetly in the direction of a painted circle, the goal. "Go byy! Paauuul!" roared Bill. A short whistle (meaning go round left) sent Paul racing in a wide arc around the three perplexed woollies. Paul crouched down, stared into the sheep's eyes then brought them 300 metres into the circle, and kept them put. He didn't bark once.

Paul was an eye-dog, a quiet shy dog able to persuade sheep with his hypnotic stare to move towards a pen or a farmer. The opposite function is that of the larger huntaways that bark the flock away. "Both dogs work differently," said Bill, giving us a crash course on dog trials. "Both are irreplaceable for us farmers". While the huntaway bark roughly means "get lost", eye dogs like Paul patiently ask "would you like to come with me sheep?"

Although the competitors and spectators are within sight and hearing distance of the trials, its only the judges who concentrate on the yelling, whistling and barking. Gossip and a couple of beers are more important at these sporting/social events.

Cartoonist Murray Ball has made another sheep dog into a national hero – his cartoon strip *Footrot Flats* tells the adventures and misadventures of "Dog" and his owner "Wal". Proof of his success is obvious from the large numbers of *Footrot Flats* posters and cartoons found in New Zealand and Australian households.

Like sheep, dogs are immigrants. Before people settled in New Zealand the only mammals were two species of bats. The first

Polynesians to come here introduced both rats and dogs. Dogs were often eaten, their meat providing rations for long journeys. When Cook anchored in Queen Charlotte Sound in 1770 he was presented with a roasted dog. The meat, he found, was equal to first grade mutton. Today New Zealand dogs are pets and working dogs only, and won't be found on the local menu!

The small town of Kaikoura on the east coast about halfway between Blenheim and Christchurch is a tourist favourite. The name means "to eat crayfish", although whale-watching has long since overtaken the attraction of a gourmet meal of cray. Forty-thousand tourists a year now take the boat trip in the hope of glimpsing the flukes of a diving sperm whale. These enormous mammals have always aroused an itching curiosity and fascination in me. As a child in Australia, I used to stare stubbornly across the ocean waiting and hoping to spot a whale.

Before we climbed into the boat for our dawn whale-watching trip, Marcus, the skipper, gave a short talk on marine biology and why the whales come to this coastline. In brief, cold and warm ocean currents meet here along the coast in a deep ocean trench, producing abundant plankton on which giant squid feed. These twelve-metre long (the length of our boat) molluscs are the sperm whales' favourite meal so they tend to congregate here.

With the use of a home-made underwater microphone our guides attempted to locate one of the submerged twenty-metre whales which have been given names like Joe, Splash, Elephant Ears or Robert Redford (whose flukes are especially handsome). Someone spotted a spout of water. "That must be Joe. It is!" For several minutes cameras and binoculars observed what looked like a wrinkly submarine on the water surface. Then its head dipped down, the moment we'd all been waiting for. In slow motion its tail flukes appeared to hang, dripping with water for a frozen moment, before the whale began its dive to depths of up to 1,600 metres.

We missed seeing a second whale, but the disappointment was fleeting as a school of dolphins suddenly began dancing about the cruising boat. At first there were just one or two but then fifty to sixty of these elegant swimmers soon appeared. The expense and early rise were really worth it.

A few hours later we reached Christchurch. Destined to be a model Anglican city, the Christchurch city plans arrived with the first settlers when they landed at Lyttelton Harbour in 1850. The passengers on board were "upright, conscientious and honest' citizens, according to the letter of recommendation they carried from their Minister. In five years, 3,549 immigrants had arrived. The initiators of the settlement, E.G. Wakefield and J.R. Godley, had selected "gentlemen farmers" that would suit a village community. In reality tough pioneers were needed who could clear bushland and live in tiny huts, surviving on meat, potatoes and bread. The dream of an ecclesiastic city was shattered. Still, a very British city remains, with cultivated parks, gothic stone architecture, rowing and cricket clubs and a willow-lined river called the Avon (honouring the Scottish river, not Shakespeare).

At the centre of the city is Cathedral Square, surrounded by offices, shops, hotels and the post office. Nowadays in the square virtually every other stall serves Asian snacks. Christchurch at times seems to be firmly in Japanese hands, and along with Rotorua and Queenstown it completes the obligatory itinerary for Japanese on one-week holidays.

At midday, droves of people swarm in the direction of Cathedral Square to hear the Wizard. Since 1970 the Aussie-born royalist and philosopher preaches and prattles to the lunchtime crowds from his stepladder. Dressed black in winter and

white in summer, he provokes everyone with speeches on any subject from God to the Queen, though feminism is a favourite.

Admittedly we really only know the wizard from hearsay because we usually let the Arts Centre steal our time when we're in Christchurch. These former university buildings were revitalised some years ago and is now a centre for theatre, arts and crafts. On Saturdays the chances are good for finding high-quality handcrafted goods or third world products. That is as long as you make it past the great smells from the dozen tiny international food stalls (Thai, Croatian, Vietnamese, Hungarian…) Sizzling, crackling steaming, mmm! It can be difficult deciding whether to start lunch with a sweet crepe or a spicy spring roll.

While a fun, striped handknitted jumper will probably go unnoticed amongst the alternatively dressed at the Arts Centre, the pinstriped blazers of the college across the road are still eyecatchers. Christ's College, founded in 1857, is one of the oldest and most prestigious private schools in New Zealand, although until the turn of the nineteenth century rich Canterbury farmers still sent their privileged sons off to private schools in England. The wearing of straw boaters at Christ's College was discontinued recently, much to the disappointment of tourists, and to the relief of long-suffering students.

While in Christchurch a brief detour to the coastal suburb of Sumner is recommended, as is the gondola ride up Mount Cavendish. In late autumn a thick brown blanket of smog hangs over the city (Christchurch still burns a lot of coal) but above the haze the snowy peaks of the Southern Alps catches the eye, and looking east are breathtaking views of Lyttelton Harbour and the countless deserted bays of Banks Peninsula.

The peninsula, named after James Cook's expedition botanist Joseph Banks, was incorrectly recorded as an island on his otherwise relatively accurate mapping of the South Island. In those days the peninsula was still forested and matai and totara from there later provided the building timber for Christchurch and Lyttelton's wharves. Fire and erosion finally cleared the forests thoroughly.

Banks Peninsula is yet another one of our favourite corners of New Zealand. In contrast to the wide flats of the Canterbury Plains, the peninsula is a wild and wind buffeted area that can be viewed from a high winding road. Not quite overgrown lava flows expose the peninsula's violent origins and narrow roads wind down to often deserted wind-sheltered bays next to the Pacific. Even in rain and fog the peninsula has a mystique as tracks and farm fences disappear into nothingness.

It was in such weather during our first visit in 1986 that a silhouette of a typical Kiwi farmer in oilskin raincoat and gumboots appeared from the fog, surrounded by his sheep and friendly dogs. The first farmer we showed the photo to in 1994 responded calmly and unsurprised, "Yeah, that's Rex my cousin." The farmer not only knew the area, he was also the curator of the museum in Okains Bay. What happened to the old shop in Pigeon Bay? Closed up!

Rex wasn't at home, but we were barely on the doormat before his wife Dorothy insisted it was tea time. "Yes, the dogs, they're all still alive, no Jenny died, but the brown shaggy one Beardie he's still going, a lovely dog." Dorothy pointed to the coat

rack, "That old oilskin, Rex can't part with the tatty thing."

The peninsula was once close to becoming French territory, and a strong French influence remains here. The French came to New Zealand in 1840 soon after the Treaty of Waitangi had been signed, too late to establish their own colony. A pity really – the Kiwi breakfast of ham, eggs, toast and instant coffee might then have been fresh croissants accompanied by huge bowls of

café au lait like you can get at Akaroa where the French established a settlement. We couldn't help wondering if the French would still have tested their nuclear bombs in the Pacific if their influence had been greater here. And how would the Kiwis and Aussies have communicated? Ooh la la mate!

Founded in 1840, Akaroa's chic, polished up "Little France" tries very hard to attract all the Francophiles it can. Picturesque,

Victorian houses on the promenade were freshly painted and the place smelt of lavender, and of course of croissants. Ooh, la la! In the Astrolabe restaurant, named after the ship of the French explorer, d'Urville, we had a delicious kumara and bacon soup, and Karl's favourite, green-lipped mussels cooked in white wine. A salad vinaigrette with a baguette was served to clean the plates.

Three passes connect the east and west coasts on the South Island: Haast Pass, Lewis Pass and Arthur's Pass. Arthur's Pass was named after Arthur Dudley Dobson, a surveyor and explorer who followed a Maori greenstone trail through the Southern Alps. The 193 kilometre road connects Greymouth on the west coast with Christchurch in the east. Originally it was built to encourage West Coast gold diggers to bring their finds to Canterbury. Today Arthur's Pass is one of the most dramatic passes in the South Island, and the train journey through the pass must be one of the highlights of any South Island trip.

An immaculate blue enveloped the morning sky above Christchurch, a perfect start for the Arthur's Pass crossing to Greymouth on the Tranzalpine Express. From reserved numbered seats the views from the spotless panoramic window were fantastic. Just before Darfield, the conductor and entertainer on board, announced "Rosie". While waiting to let a coal train through, the steward took our leftover pies out to the platform. And as she does every day, Rosie, a 17-year-old dog, came to collect her pies. Rosie is a walking advertisement for railway pies (well waddling at least) and an officially recognised tourist attraction. The community will probably erect a monument in her memory, and the railways a concrete pie. Past Sheffield and Springfield the train wound in broad curves up the mountains above the Canterbury Plains and the sun soon disappeared.

The towering clouds should have warned us. The Southern Alps are the South Island's weather divide and not far from Arthur's Pass it began to rain. In the last and open carriage it began to get uncomfortable. Diesel smoke, an icy wind and finally a pitch-black tunnel drove us all back into the dining carriage. Morning tea and complimentary sandwiches warmed everyone up. Our neighbours were a couple of Japanese teenagers: "We arrived yesterday"; two Americans on a forty-day world trip: "We're flying on to Sydney tomorrow," and an Australian farming couple: "We come every year for two months to Christchurch".

Beyond the 8.6 kilometre Otira tunnel the sky was blue-black. West coast weather. With 5,000 millimetres of rain annually, it has to fall sometime. Otira is a collection of faded wooden houses behind a freshly painted railway station. In Greymouth the rain gushes down. A one hour stop is just enough for a cappuccino and a ten-minute sprint through the former coal mining town that tourism has brought to life. Rain doesn't flatter the largest town on the West Coast, instead it verifies its name. Thank goodness we didn't encounter "The Barber", a wind as icy and sharp as a barber's razor.

East Coast

Back on the east coast, the weather couldn't have been better. Near Timaru State Highway 1 leaves the Canterbury Plains and follows the coast. When we headed southwards in 1986 and drove through Timaru, all the country's economic problems seemed to have accumulated there. It was all to do with sheep. While 2,000 freezing works (abattoir) employees boycotted the loading of live sheep bound for Mexico, 5,000 farmers demonstrated against the union's blockade and the government. Not without difficulty, a few hundred police attempted to keep the opposing sides apart.

It was a trial run to transport 17,000 live sheep by ship, a method frequently used in Australia. The torturous animal transport had also drawn opposition from animal rights activists who joined the abattoir workers. The latter believed that their 30,000 strong union would be threatened if lambs continued to be shipped overseas for slaughter. The farmers' interest however was in selling their stock, either deep frozen or alive and kicking.

Rain dispersed the harbour workers who took shelter by the fast food vans and buses. "Job Exporter!" declared the freezing workers on their banners. "I am against live sheep export!" The union boss gave a fiery speech, but the major theme of the day was the strike for a fifteen per cent pay rise. They had been striking for weeks.

"Why do you need more pay?" yelled a farmer above their heads, "with your $500 a week you earn three times as much as us!" The farmer's gripe was also against government. They felt cheated by the government, and saw only bleak prospects: "No farmers, no future!" Almost daily the local papers were reporting young farmers being bankrupted by twenty-eight per cent interest rates and halved profits. "We can't pay our bills!" they complained, to which city dwellers retorted "You've never had to pay them!" They were partly right too.

From 1984 the newly elected Labour Government began cutting subsidies that had allowed farmers to live way above realistic wool and mutton market values. New Zealand was no longer Mother England's backyard farm. On entering the European Common Market, Britain bought from its neighbours. It was a blow that Kiwis wrestled to overcome, as they slipped down the ladder of affluence. In the 1950s New Zealand was said to be "living off the sheep's back", and after the USA and Canada, was the world's third wealthiest nation. In 1965 New Zealand ranked eighth on per capita income, but by the end of the 1980s had slipped further down to 25th place. In 1994, however, they were back at number 18.

Eighty kilometres south of Timaru is the town Oamaru, which means "a place to dry meat." and probably relates to the times hundreds of years ago when Maori hunted the flightless moa on the South Canterbury plains. The harbour town of Oamaru is famous for its limestone buildings. The soft, white, porous building material is quarried in the area. The stone, which can be cut with a saw and sometimes even a knife, hardens after being cut and stored in the open. It is ideal for fancy scroll work on Corinthian pillars with which so many of the neo-classical facades are decorated.

I was searching for Eden Street. The first volume of Janet Frame's autobiography is set in her childhood home in Oamaru during the 1930s. The New Zealander, Jane Campion produced a moving film, *An Angel at my Table,* based on Frame's astounding life story. It is a portrait of the very shy red-haired Janet, who, after being wrongly diagnosed spent several nightmare years in a psychiatric institution. A literature prize saved her at the last minute from a lobotomy.

Thirty-eight kilometres further south of Oamaru is a geological curiosity worth stopping for. The Moeraki Boulders started "growing" some sixty million years ago as salts accumulated in layers around a core. These spherical oddities weigh several tonnes and measure up to four metres in diameter. Unfortunately only those too heavy to be carried away for garden decoration remain on the beach. Legends say that they are the round food baskets that went overboard from the ancestral canoe Arai-te-uru from Hawaiki. The baskets, filled with kumara, were washed ashore and turned to stone.

Scottish settlers arrived in Otago Harbour in 1848 to found a new centre which they called *Dunedin,* the ancient Gaelic name of their home capital, Edinburgh. Here too settlers arrived with town plans and street names in their baggage. As devout Scottish Presbyterians they saw a chance to establish a city of "piety, diligence, and honesty". As far as traditions go Dunedin has remained somewhat Scottish. The Scots poet, Robert Burns, welcomes visitors to the Octagon from his monument. The capital of Otago holds an annual Highland Games, distils its own whisky and even has a kiltmaker. During the goldrush of the 1860s (within two years the population grew from 12,000 to 60,000) Dunedin became New Zealand's financial centre and its richest city.

Dunedin lies at the end of a twenty kilometre long natural harbour. Captain Cook missed it but it was later found by whalers and sealers. A round tour of Otago Peninsula is mandatory. A snaking lower coast road leads to the royal albatross colony at Taiaroa Head, and a high road opens up a panorama across a ridge to Dunedin. Across the harbour is Port Chalmers from where the historic first frozen shipments of lamb and mutton left for Europe. New Zealand's entry into international trade had begun with a disaster: the depression of 1878, in which the major London banks collapsed and the price of wheat and wool hit rock bottom. The wizard that lifted New Zealand's hopes was a ship called the *Dunedin,* a refrigerated ship that sailed in February

Protesting freezer workers, Timaru Harbour

1882 from Port Chalmers with dairy products and frozen goods on board. The Europeans were at once convinced of the quality, and thus began a prosperous frozen meat industry that raised New Zealand's affluence to one of the highest in the world.

South of Dunedin, the Catlins is one of those regions of New Zealand that is often bypassed. Our insider tip: drive there with a full tank only – service stations are rare sights along the unsealed road. This isolated coastal strip was named after Edward Cattlin, an Australian whaler. Bizarre steep coastal cliffs, fantastic sweeping deserted sandy beaches, waterfalls, old podocarp forests of rimu, kamahi, rata and totara trees are all found in this almost forgotten corner. The back road drive between Balclutha and Invercargill is well worth the detour for a few days in any season.

The campground at Kaka Point was closed in autumn so we parked at a turnoff just five metres from the beach. Traffic: two vehicles during the whole night. View: the storm-battered lighthouse at Nugget Point. The lighthouse is the oldest continually used lighthouse in New Zealand, a lonely tower watching over rugged surf-washed cliffs. The Nuggets are a dozen craggy islands that jut into the sea breaking waves in front of the promontory.

Scrambling up a hillside we looked for shelter from the wind to watch the wildlife with our binoculars. We searched in vain for yellow-eyed penguins, but saw sea lions shuffling up to uncomfortable looking peaks of rocks. Elephant seals had to be content heaving their several tonne bodies

onto the stony beach below. Instead of the hour planned, we stayed until sunset. Somewhere out there was the South Pole, and in between was nothing but water, ice and a few desolate islands.

Heading further south we reached the most southerly region of New Zealand, Southland. The capital here is Invercargill, another town with Scottish roots and streets named after Scottish rivers. The Scots must have felt quite at home in this rainy and stormy corner of the island. Invercargill is high on the list of statistics for unemployment, and is often not on itiner-

aries of tour agencies. The clock ticks a little slower here – in May the Christmas decorations were still hanging across the street. With its impressive Victorian facades, arcades and cafés, Invercargill has no need to be shy.

Still further south is Bluff, New Zealand's "Land's End". The flood of lights that appear to be a city comes from Tiwai Point, one of the world's largest aluminium smelters. Bluff however is just a one side of a street parallel to the railway line and beach. A pub and a few stores are bracketed by a

milk bar at each end of the road. On a Thursday night at the end of the world the fish and chip shop in the main street is obviously the place to be for dinner. The chalkboard menu outside tempted with not only butterfish but a heap of oysters, chips and salad for $15. As deep fried oysters go they tasted good.

Customers came in, called out their order at the door and then disappeared to wait in their car parked directly outside. "Friday evening is all hell loose in here. That's really fish and chip day. The Catholics brought the tradition with them and it stuck," chuckled Mike. "A few folk come every day, maybe they don't have a cooker at home!" I shiver at the thought. Then I too wouldn't fit into my jogging trousers any more.

The television news was on in the background above the tables. Thumper, the one legged kiwi (bird) was on his way to recovery, reported the news reader. One of these flightless, night birds had been hit by a vehicle near Milford Sound. For the necessary amputation Thumper was flown all the way to Palmerston North. The next report was from London where a survivor of a flesh-eating virus showed us his leg. Finally, cricket, rugby and the weather.

In Bluff we have an address to visit. One of my mother's golfing friends in Perth, Australia, said we should visit her parents. "Fred and Myrtle would love to see you, they live in the most southerly house in New Zealand." It's not quite correct about the southernmost house, but they were delighted with our visit. Busloads of visitors come nearly every day to see their paua house with its wall to wall covering of paua shells, better known as abalone in other parts of the world. Fred and Myrtle are genuine down under personalities known to nearly every Kiwi after they and their paua house appeared in a television bread commercial.

Paua meat is not only considered a delicacy, but the blue and green opal-like shimmering shell is also both beautiful and valuable. Maori used the shell for jewellery decoration. But here the shells were used as a wall covering. Cheekily, Fred points to one of the thousands of shells, "See that one there! I don't like that one at all!". After a well-rehearsed pause, he explains, "This whole jolly business began with that very shell!" It's easy to tell 90-year-old Fred really enjoys telling his life story. The two of them ran the local milk bar for over twenty-two years. In 1994 their proud family statistics were: eight children, twenty-nine grandchildren and twenty-two great grandchildren. Christmas can be a nightmare.

A second bus parked in front of the bright blue house which was guarded by a concrete moa. This time it was a school bus from Wellington. Entry is free but they do have a donation box and they sell postcards.

Sheep, sheep..

Easter Friday, six in the morning. The weather forecast for Southland was promising a good day. Slowly, almost at walking pace, Graham lifted the helicopter out of

Autumn muster in the Garvie Mountains

171

the thick ground fog in the Waikaia valley. We have only the absolute necessities with us: warm clothes, two cameras, film, sleeping bags.

We had met Sharky, the manager of Glenaray, New Zealand's largest sheep station, by chance. The recommendation had come from a fisherman who knocked on our frost covered tent to invite us for morning tea. Sharky, who's in his mid fifties, fitted the image we had of the quintessential New Zealander: sun-weathered face and hands, unshaven, checked woollen shirt, heavy woollen work trousers, reserved and completely unflappable. "If you've time," he suggested, "come back in three weeks, then we'll be driving the wethers back down to the farm." We had time!

Every Easter at Glenaray nine men with sixty dogs and six pack horses depart for the remote Garvie Mountains. For two weeks Jack Mack's Hut serves as their base for one of the largest operations of this sort: the autumn muster of 14,000 wethers (castrated rams) out of the high country down to winter pastures belonging to the long established Pinckney family.

The team had already been in the hills for ten days, and were hut bound due to bad weather. Supplies were coming to an end.

"Two bottles of rum will just bang together, better to bring a whole box, just to keep them tidy," Jake, cook and packer said when he'd radioed the SOS back to the farm.

Potatoes, cabbage and coal were permitted by old Miss Pinckney, but not the "box". After several kilometres we reached a concrete bridge where Graham pulled the chopper to the left across green fields and small clumps of trees and up to the slopes of the high country. After a few minutes we passed over Bush Hut, a corrugated iron building below the tree line, and twenty minutes later we arrived at Jack Mack's hut. We descended into another world, wild inaccessible high country, blanketed by metre-high tussock grass.

Karl has been drawn to the open tussock country used for grazing sheep and cattle ever since our first visit to the Antipodes. Much of the grazing land in New Zealand exists at the expense of native forest cover which was cleared by both Maori and Pakeha. Two hundred years ago, fifty per cent of the country was covered in evergreen forest – barely a quarter of the native cover remains now. Burnoffs by Maori and forest clearing by European settlers sacrificed the vegetation for the monoculture of sheep. In ecological terms it has been a catastrophe, a high price for playing the role of British farm in the South Pacific.

The four sheep that Cook landed here survived just a few days. It was not until sixty years later that merinos were imported from neighbouring Australia, and by the turn of the century there were fourteen mil-

Day's end, musterers at Bush Hut

lion of them. Today the romney has over-taken the merino; it carries less wool, but reaches a killing age much faster. A romney-merino cross has proven to be the most robust breed, able to withstand the raw high country climate.

Jack Mack's, a timber and iron high country hut, has tradition. Old pin-ups of young 1950s beauties still hang under the roof, and on the beams are scratched the names of previous mustering teams going back to the 1930s. At the head of the forty square-metre hut are the stove and shelves of supplies, at the other end are the bunks, and in between is a long rough wooden table and benches. Anton, at twenty, the youngest of the team, showed us his grandfather's name on one of the beams. He had been head shepherd thirty years ago. Like most of the men Anton is a permanent employee of Glenaray, but Terry and Ray are neighbouring farmers for whom the autumn muster is a paid holiday with cowboy romantic and a little adventure, probably one of the last of its kind in New Zealand.

The boys hardly noticed our arrival despite the whining of the helicopter engine. Without looking over the edge of their cards they mumbled an obligatory "g'day" and remain distant. Our visit has broken a hut tradition: I'm the first female to join a muster. But as there were no spare bunks in the cosy hut we had to sleep in the nearby saddle hut in temperatures below zero between sweaty saddles and sacks of oats and hay.

For two days the men had been confined to the hut by fog and sleet. Twice a day they interrupted their card game of 500 to feed the horses and dogs. Dog tucker lies on top of a huge boulder known as Dead Horse Rock – access is by a shaky wooden ladder. Every year an old pack horse ends up on top of this rock.

From the air the treeless high country looks as if it's covered with a soft golden carpet. Tussock, a tough bushy grass, reaches one and a half metres high and can grow on infertile stony ground. Without a good horse it is impossible to make progress through this stubborn grass, and even four wheel drives have no chance. Rocks, razor sharp speargrass and knee-deep holes make it almost impossible to go by foot in some places. So into the saddle! Karl just managed to survive his first horse ride in over twenty-five years for two reasons. His horse was called Fuller. Why? "Any fuller and she'd burst!" On top of that she was pregnant and unable to make large strides in steep country. With fog and low cloud moving in again, we returned after two hours anyway.

By the time we got back, Jake, ex-butcher and "chief of tucker", had peeled the last kilo of red skinned potatoes and swept the hut while meat cooked in the old Orion coal range. Like the oven, many things in Jake's kitchen were antiques, like the large biscuit tin that old Miss Pinckney filled with

Pack-horses at Jack Mack's Hut

a ration of creamy white honey, and the tower of Imperial Toilet Paper rolls from the 1930s, crisp and yellowed, that she makes the men take each year.

"Must be about five o'clock already!" The men began mumbling that it could be that time now. Skip stood up, went to the store-room with a key and returned with a peppermint green bottle. Rum time! Not a booze up, more a ritual. Inner Circle rum. Eleven large half-pint enamel mugs were lined up on the table and Skip dispensed equal measures (three schnapps glasses per mug) of eighty-five per cent proof rum into the mugs. The rum was topped with raspberry soda from a white plastic soda stream that both quenched the firewater and made it drinkable. The pre-dinner drink was savoured slowly over a game of cards. That was their lot.

The rum loosened tongues and stories became more fantastic. "Do you remember last year the fog was so thick, we all saddled the wrong horses?"; "And John went off without his dogs Nip, Ned and Kink and came back without any sheep?" Ray squints a look at us. How much do we believe? Every year they'll sit here with new stories. "You remember that kraut on Fuller, how he nearly fell in the creek with all his cameras?" and they'll laugh just like they did then.

As the only female (and an Aussie at that) they enjoyed pulling my leg. I had learnt how to survive amongst characters like these in my two years as a governess in the Australian outback. ("In the bush when you open your mouth – exaggerate!") "How do like your rum, Jackie?". "The rum's fine

but the raspberry sure burns holes in your socks." They laugh and I am accepted.

The kerosene lamp hissed quietly and at seven o'clock Jake served "tea". First course is a cauliflower soup served in the now empty rum mugs. Green beans, boiled potatoes, and the most tender roast mutton that we'd ever had were piled up on white enamel plates with a blue edge. Jake had cooked the mutton with a few herbs on the old stove for three hours. Yesterday the table cloth was a yellowed 1981 newspaper, now it was the latest, brought in by the heli-

copter along with the supplies. Just for once world politics strayed into the wilderness.

Our second night at Jack Mack's was clear, starry, frosty and uncomfortable. At 4.30 a.m. we heard Jake lighting the stove and an hour later he started preparing breakfast. Terry herded the horses together. A few brave souls washed themselves in the icy creek; we just brushed our teeth. Breakfast was steak, eggs, a few tomatoes, thick slices of cheddar and mountains of toast. The coffee was heaven after the freezing night.

For three days we hadn't seen a single sheep, except for the mutton chops on our plates. There were two sheep for every three hectares of grazing land and the musterers had to find all the sheep in 20,000 hectares of land. When it's foggy they don't even start looking. Over a week the musterers had rounded the sheep together in wide arcs driving them out from hidden dips, over hillcrests and ridges. Now at last came "The Big Day!". "We'll give it a go!" said Skip, signalling the departure. Among the men there were shouts and cries like children, and the dogs barked, jumped and yowled. Earlier Skip had taken the helicopter up to have a look. He gave each man a beat, a few tips and times that they should keep to.

The high point of the two week muster is the crossing where all 14,000 sheep come together as one big mob and are driven through a narrow fence opening across the shallow Gorge Creek. First all we heard was barking dogs, and an hour later we saw the first sheep, appearing in ones and twos, then small groups, then in long strings. Finally the mob appeared over the hilltop like an advancing army.

Skip positioned himself and his dogs at a critical viewpoint. Sharky had the right flank covered, usually an easy position when the sheep follow the flow. A group of twenty sheep however tried to make a getaway up the valley, led by two woollies with extra long wool that escaped last season's shearing. "They know what freedom means," Sharky laughed "but they know too well how cold it can get up here too." Then he roared "Get in behiiiind Ted!" A long, drawn out whistle was effective. Ted circled the dropouts with long strides and drove them back to the mob.

Before crossing the creek the mob was divided into smaller mobs to avoid a panic when they're driven through the small temporary fence opening. In an unbroken flow they swarmed down the almost vertical drop to Gorge Creek and up the opposite side which was just as steep. From a distance they looked like maggots crawling up an animal's back as they disappeared over the ridge.

In the evening we went down to Bush Hut. Three men would retrace the area to clear out a few getaways Skip had spotted from the helicopter. Then the muster would be all over for another year. The wind from the helicopter blades blew horse blankets from the fence and tired men back into their hut. We threw our packs into the back of the chopper, Ted and Kink jumped in after them, and we lifted off. Eight minutes later we landed behind the farm's new shearing shed.

From Glenaray it's just a couple of miles to the few houses in Waikaia, or to Gore, the next town. On our way to Gore we came upon a type of aircraft I thought had long since died out. The sight of two Tiger Moth biplanes being rolled out onto a field, caused us to stop in our tracks. "Test flights of new Moths," explained the men leaning on the fence. This ageless flying machine made from timber and aluminium where the pilot sits uncovered (like a motorcyclist), was used by the Royal Air Force as a training machine in the World War II and was produced by the thousand.

New Zealanders have a special relationship to flying. Many Kiwis are convinced that their own countryman Richard Pearse had an aircraft airborne in 1902, a year before the Wright brothers. These days single propeller machines are standard transport on isolated farms.

Today, Tiger Moths are built here in Mandeville by Colin Smith. Inside the hangar looks more like a museum than a factory, being filled with biplanes as full of fantasy as their names suggest: Gypsy Moth, Fox Moth, Dragon and Puss Moth. New "Moths" are built with fibreglass and other high-tech materials. Old machines are restored according to original plans, complete with wooden propellers and morse-code machines set in brass.

We have a friend in common. A few days earlier Gus Watson had called Colin from Queenstown to discuss construction plans for a biplane. Nothing unusual in that, except that Gus is confined to a wheelchair. Karl met Gus in 1983 when he was photographing houses designed by Ian Athfield. Gus lives in one of Athfield's houses, one of the loveliest houses that we know. It's nothing luxurious, rather an enlargement of a once tiny log cabin that he built with rough birch beams and lots of timber. The

Workshop for bi-planes, Mandeville

extensions were designed by Athfield after the crippling skiing accident that left Gus in a wheelchair.

Gus lives independently in an out of way valley below Coronet Peak. He is a fighter, still a bit of a daredevil and his positive nature and love of life is well above the average person's. Gus is not handicapped as such. He drives a car, goes flying and boating with friends when possible, and was on a tropical island with his young daughter Milly last time we visited. Today he is a well known local artist in the Queenstown area, selling water colour paintings faster than he can paint, so he says!

Queenstown, New Zealand's most successful tourist trap, is surrounded by 2,000 metre high mountains on the shores of the picturesque Lake Wakatipu. Nerve-rattling jet boating, bungy jumping, rent-a-tent, white-water rafting, mountain biking, heli-skiing, steamboat trips, pizzas, tacos, sushi – this one time gold prospectors' nest offers everything a touring spirit desires. From goldrush to adrenaline rush. The ideal is to equip oneself with waterproof trousers, maps, weather reports and get out quickly to the great outdoors.

The choice of tramping routes in the south-west is great too, with the Milford, Hollyford, Rees-Dart, Kepler, Greenstone, Caples and Routeburn tracks all found nearby. The latter is on the edge of the two national parks, Mount Aspiring and Fiordland National Park.

Routeburn

"The Glenorchy road is closed until this afternoon due to flooding" wasn't the report that would entice us from our warm beds at 5 a.m. on the morning we wanted to start the Routeburn Track. We'd been ready to go for two days, but the weather forecast was horrible. A low pressure system battered moist westerly winds against the Southern Alps, forcing airmasses to rise and drop their load mercilessly over Fiordland. This was quite normal. Eight metres of rain falls annually in Milford Sound, while Glenorchy on the other side of the Main Divide at the start of the Routeburn receives a mere 1,100 millimetres yearly.

The Christmas floods of 1993 even hit the European news. In January 153.7 millimetres of rain were recorded within twenty-four hours at Glenorchy. On the Routeburn, the storm destroyed twelve footbridges and washed away parts of the track. But by the end of March the army had repaired the track, cleared fallen trees and rebuilt bridges. Tramping is an important business in New Zealand.

Finally, at the first hint of the rain easing up, we were sitting in the six o'clock Backpackers Express, a vintage bone-shaker bus that transports dozens of trampers seventy-five kilometres to Glenorchy and the starting point of several tracks.

As we started around midday from Routeburn Shelter it began to rain. But who could complain? What's a rainforest without rain? Without rain there'd be no moss, lichens or waterfalls. In an evergreen beech forest, we trod past dripping moss-covered trees, crossed the Sugarloaf Stream on a narrow swaying swingbridge, and felt our faces being wiped by cool moist fern fronds. I had dreamed of this for the past year.

Two hours later we crossed grassy flats beside the crystal clear waters of the Route Burn (burn being Scots for small stream) where smoke from the first hut at Routeburn Flats was visible. After four more hours we reached the Routeburn Falls and the second hut, Falls hut. These huts are exceptionally comfortable, and between October and mid May have mattresses, toilets, gas and water.

The next morning we began the slow climb to the Harris Saddle. Wooden boardwalks assisted our progress through fragile swampy ground and protected the flora at the same time. The path wound steeply upwards, and Lake Harris suddenly appeared before us, a black shimmering lake surrounded by green-gold hills and wet black cliffs. A Scottish oil painting in New Zealand.

Harris Saddle lies 1,277 metres above sea level and is the highest point of the trail. Black glowering clouds hovered like predators, and in such weather the climb to Conical Hill above the track is not on the agenda, however spectacular the panorama may be. In winter (May–October) the saddle is often impassable due to snow and avalanche danger. Even in summer care is necessary. Above the treeline a turn of weather and insufficient clothing can be life threatening. "Fiordland weather," a damp tramper wrote in a hut log book, "comes the day before it is forecast."

From Routeburn Shelter at the start of the track we had crossed three climatic and vegetation zones and now found ourselves on the weather divide approaching one of the wettest regions on earth, Fiordland. We dug out our rain capes. It rained. Just above the treeline a small path named Deadmans Tack dropped into the Hollyford Valley. Our map offered a brief, clear description of this alternative – steep and direct. We stayed on the higher path.

Three hours later a gap in the swirling cloud and moist fog allowed a glimpse down to Lake Mackenzie. It's green waters were set in a stony hollow surrounded by rata trees, and in one corner was our goal, Mackenzie hut. A zigzag path led 300 metres down to the lake through a fairytale forest draped with mosses. We clambered over giant fallen trees, twisted roots and slippery moss-covered rocks. When we entered Mackenzie hut it smelled of damp woollens and warm noodles. At 1,036 metres it has fifty-three bunks, cooking and toilet facilities. The heart of this relatively luxurious Department of Conservation hut was the communal room where a tiny coal-fired stove struggled to dry twenty-five pairs of sodden boots and socks and warm as many people.

The tramp through the clouds was rewarded next morning with spectacular views up to Emily Peak and the snowcapped Darran Mountains on the other side of the Hollyford valley. But before the sun's rays

penetrated our valley at ten o'clock we unpacked the rain gear once again. Remember, this is rainforest!

From Lake Mackenzie to The Divide on the Milford Road is about ten kilometres, or three hours hike. Many begin the Routeburn from The Divide, but it doesn't matter which direction you walk the track. With enough time and food and if blisters have not yet appeared, then it is worth continuing along the Caples Track back towards Glenorchy. In 1863 the gold prospector Patrick Caples explored this route, eventually linking Lake Wakatipu with the west coast at Martins Bay. He was the first European to make the journey, though Maori had earlier penetrated these valleys while searching for and trading in greenstone.

About an hour beyond Howden hut an intersection on the Greenstone Track marked the Caples Track. The Caples was supposed to be a little more strenuous, but we were surprised that we were the only ones headed for the Upper Caples hut just six hours away. Those continuing along the Greenstone wished us "Good luck! It's straight up!" The Kiwis probably knew best.

The map showed a 300 metre rise between the river bed to the saddle. We clambered over tree roots and fallen logs, this time as slippery as ice after all the rain. There was no real track and our feet didn't find an even piece of ground until we were at the saddle. Thank goodness little red and white markers the size of beer mats were nailed to the trees and not yet overgrown

Swing bridge above Sugarloaf Stream

with moss. It was dark, wet and oh so steep with a backpack! I used a beech stick which saved my short legs. Soaked with sweat we reached McKellar Saddle. Here there was a wonderful moor, alpine flowers, and of course being above the trees at 945 metres, a fantastic view of densely forested mountains and not a soul in sight. The Caples River has its source here, and we followed the river, downhill of course through beech forest and past waterfalls. Landslide paths and the occasional tangle of fallen trees reminded us of the 153.7 millimetres of rain in twenty-four hours. We got to the hut just before dark and only half the bunks were taken. But there is an abundance of hungry sandflies. The Caples huts are smaller and simpler than those on the Routeburn, with no gas cookers.

Our last day was an easy walk along the broad open river valley of the Caples. Beyond mid-Caples hut some of the land is grazed. The weather was perfect, the river full and the walking was easy as we were headed out to catch a one o'clock bus. We arrived with time to eat the rest of our food and wash our feet before the bus took us to our boat which shot us across Lake Wakatipu back to Glenorchy. The local café seemed to expect our arrival and we enjoyed freshly baked quiches, sourdough bread and a cappuccino. "I hear the Rees and Dart track is one of the best tracks for mountain views…" and so the next walk was already being planned.

Fiordland

In no other country do the contrasts lie so near to one another than in the islands of New Zealand: rainforest, glaciers, geysers, kilometres of black beaches, volcanoes and fertile farmland. A country of superlatives, equalled only by the descriptions in the guidebooks: the oldest, the deepest, the most beautiful, the hottest, the most isolated, the world's only, the wettest…

Fiordland is no exception. New Zealand's largest National Park (1.2 million hectares) counts as one of the true wilderness regions on the planet. But there's little there for sun worshippers! The region ranks as one of the wettest on earth with an unbelievable eight (yes eight) metres of rain falling here each year. Maybe that was what so fascinated us. Of all the misfortunes we arrived at Milford Sound in sunshine. "The visitors here all pray for sunshine and a calm boat trip," said the boat's guide shaking his head "but that's the worst thing that can happen." Storms and rain transform the sheer stone cliffs into spectacular walls of water. "When it rains she's a beauty that's for sure."

Milford Sound, once described as the "the eighth wonder of the world" is still Fiordland's main attraction. More mysterious dark and remote, though nonetheless accessible, is Doubtful Sound, one of fourteen major fiords that reach far inland in the south-west of the South Island.

Visiting Doubtful Sound involves a journey in several stages. First is a boat journey over Lake Manapouri. Morning fog hung threateningly over the lake, trees on the banks were almost black, the water with its silver shimmer even blacker. Two hundred days a year, according to the statistics, are rainy days. And this was without doubt going to be one of them. Still, twenty people have gathered for the trip in spite of (or maybe because of) the weather. In the nearby shop toasted sandwiches and snacks were being purchased at the last minute as passengers discovered no meals were available on board. The catamaran takes an hour to cross Lake Manapouri. "We our now 780 metres above sea level … at 433 metres deep the second deepest…". The lake with a hundred islands, as the Maori named it, was the subject of one the greatest environmental controversies in the country. Plans to raise the water level by eleven metres for hydro-electricity generation brought a quarter of a million signature petition protest. As a result the scheme went ahead but water levels were maintained at normal levels and the lake and its forests saved.

From the boat a bus collected us for the drive along a gravel road (once the service road for the dam workers) up to Wilmot Pass and over to the sound. A two-minute photo stop on top of the pass wasn't enough to savour the spectacular view down to Doubtful Sound. The name was given by Captain Cook who was afraid he wouldn't be able to sail out again.

It rained, but that didn't matter. On the contrary, we were lucky! Forests and rivers are magical when their thirst is quenched. Long beards of lichen drooped from moss-covered, dripping beech trees; swirling mist blurred the edges between land, water and sky; sprays from waterfalls were delightfully refreshing.

On Doubtful Sound we cruised for three hours to reach the open ocean. We hoped and waited for the dolphins that usually guide the boat. The captain took the boat up into a small side bay and switched off the motor to let us hear the power of the "sounds of silence." We were impressed, even without dolphins.

In this part of the world introduced opossums and deer are the greatest enemy of wilderness. European settlers weren't content with introducing domestic and working animals such as sheep, cattle and horses. They weren't prepared to go without hedgehogs, rabbits, and possums. The number of possums in New Zealand is estimated at seventy million – at least. The government as well as conservationists are predicting an horrific catastrophe.

Without any natural predators, red deer, released in 1851 as a game animal bred out of control. By 1956 they were officially considered vermin. To save the native vegetation a bounty was put on the animals to reduce their numbers and hopefully kill them off completely in national parks. Deer hunting became attractive as export demand (Germany is the biggest buyer) grew and a deer farming industry was established. But the work begun by hunters on foot with guns and traps has now largely been taken over by the "chopper boys" with helicopters.

In 1986 we had an appointment with Dick and Jeff, two of the original chopper boys, somewhere at a hut between Manapouri and Te Anau. Dick Deaker ran a helicopter company with his partner Hannibal Hayes in those days. In winter they flew heli-skiers up to the highest snow fields in the Southern Alps, and at other times they hunted red deer.

After a jolting two-hour ride we found the fishing hut that served as a base for flights into southern Fiordland. It was dark when we heard them approach. The thumping of the advancing helicopter sounded threatening in the still of night. A spotlight searched the ground, a load of deer in hanging in blue plastic beneath the chopper was lowered to the ground, and then the machine landed. Dick refuelled the chopper. Jeff, his business partner and shooter, was dressed in a yellow jumpsuit smeared with blood, and his crash helmet was a reminder

The hunt with helicopters is dangerous

that his job is not without danger. He untangled the deer from the net, strapped it up with a leather belt and pulled it to a trailer.

The evening meal was already prepared. A pot of beef (Dick and Jeff prefer beef) had been simmering for hours, and the potatoes and cabbage were soon cooked. Everything was covered in butter and Worcestershire sauce. We don't get much of a chance to chat as both men were dead tired and fell into bed directly after the meal.

At five in the morning a tinny alarm clock rattled us out of our sleep. A few hasty steps on the gravel outside signal that the day had begun. My feet were hardly on the ground when the whine and whirr of the big bird starting up came with a deafening shock. Woollen hat, gloves, camera, film? I hurried outside and Jeff greeted me with ear muffs. I ducked under the rotor blades and heaved myself into the rear compartment.

This was my first flight in a helicopter and the thick fog wasn't very encouraging. Dick, in his blue down jacket and green headphones, had to lean half out of the machine to see better. Where the two hunters sat there were no doors anyway. For about ten minutes we felt our way upstream until Dick found a hole in the bank of fog. Under full power the chopper was lifted out of the fog into a crisp clear steely blue sky tinged with pink in the east. With great ease we climbed steep hills and playfully glided over a rocky saddle and down into the neighbouring valley.

In the distance shimmering skins of fiords blinked and reflected amongst the dark landmasses. One of these was probably Dusky Sound by the Tasman Sea. We hovered above mountain lakes and stony cliffs, and dark beech forests and rata bearded with bright lichen contrasted with open moor landscapes and brown tussock grasslands.

After an hour in the air above New Zealand's wildest remote corner, nothing particular has happened (it was a working day after all). Dick and Jeff haven't said a word to one another, they both stare downwards.

Then suddenly and without warning, Dick pulled the machine round in a tight curve. My stomach doesn't seem to make the curve. Jeff grabbed his net gun. Beneath us three deer were on the run stirred out of hiding by the noisy bird of prey. In a zigzag the agile Hughes 500 followed the bounty from barely ten metres above. Jeff pulled the trigger, and, like a ghostly hand, a four square-metre net fell over one of the deer bringing it to the ground. The empty casing flew into the back, hitting me in the shoulder, and the next net was fixed on the gun.

With the introduction of helicopters deer hunters had to experiment. After unsuccessful attempts at shooting tranquilisers, net guns, developed on the West Coast, proved a success. The weighted nets are folded and taped into canisters which are shot from a special gun which shoots the spreading net over a fleeing animal. Chasing deer is dangerous work in a helicopter which must dive into tiny clearings, and operate near steep hill faces.

The next ghostly hand spreads out just to the side of the animal which drags the net behind it. Dick lowers the chopper as near as possible to the slope. From three metres Jeff jumped out onto the tussock grass, snatched the net and the quarry with lightning speed before pulling himself onto the chopper's runner.

The third animal, a six pointer, lay in the tussock after two shots with a .308 semi-automatic rifle. Only does are caught alive. Minutes later we landed in a clearing to gather the animals together. While Jeff heaved them across, Dick gutted the buck and I tried to forget my sea-sickness. Before my dizziness can stabilise I'm back in the storage space, sharing it now with a deer.

If the deer survive the shock of the hunt it becomes a breeding animal for the deer farming business. There is high demand for venison because of its low fat content and freedom from contamination and chemical substances. In the early 1980s hunters could get up to $4,000 for a female deer, but prices have plummeted and with the expense of running a helicopter, hunting is not so lucrative. Today, carrying tourists over Fiordland or above the Southern Alps is more profitable.

A scenic flight from Te Anau is to be recommended. Despite the expense, a flight over the alpine meadows and lakes and fiords of this World Heritage Park has more variety in our opinion than a flight over Mt Cook. Of course we wouldn't want to dissuade anyone from a cooling trip up to New Zealand's highest mountain. Not at all, as we too took a dragonfly-like plane, a Piper Cherokee, for an unforgettable flight up to the peaks and glaciers of the snow-clad Mount Cook National Park.

As if we couldn't get enough, another unforgettable trip was our clamber up to Mueller Hut. "Clear as a barrel!" was the weather report from the park ranger as we prepared to ascend from the Hooker valley the 1,000 metres to Mueller hut. First there is a steep climb through the bush, then gravelly slopes to the tiny corrugated-iron hut held to the ground by steel ropes. For us it was just a short trip into the area, but the other occupants were on week-long mountain climbing trips. We were laden with plasters and chocolate and they with ice-axes and ropes!

Enlivened by the distant thunders of ice avalanches and the panorama of a peach coloured Aoraki, our meal (sardines, rice and tomato sauce) tasted even more fantastic. The next morning we were enveloped in a thick porridge of fog.

Although New Zealand's highest mountain lost ten metres from its summit in a recent spectacular landslide, it is still 3,754 metres high. Aoraki, as the Maori call it, is shrouded in legends. One legend tells of the crew of the Arai-te-uru canoe that came from Hawaiki, and went inland after being shipwrecked. Aoraki, a small boy who sat on his grandfather's shoulder saw the mountain first which was then named after this youngest newcomer. Another story from Maori mythology tells of four brothers, ancestors of the sky father Rangi and

the earth mother Papa, who came to earth in their mythical canoes. Their boat became the South Island and the four brothers the mountains.

After many detours we eventually arrived on the west coast. Whether in Ireland, Scotland, Alaska or Patagonia, somehow it is always the west coast not the east that attracts. From Haast in the south, to Westport 435 kilometres away in the north, a well-built road follows the coast though forests, fields and swamps.

West Coast

During the goldrush 130 years ago almost 40,000 people (mostly men) lived along the West Coast. Today there are 30,000 Coasters prepared to cope with or enjoy the elements. Graham, the helicopter pilot at Waikaia, had given us the address of the Shaw brothers. Well, calling it an address is saying a bit much, especially when its simply "Gillespies Beach, West Coast". But because the Coast is so sparsely populated everyone knows everyone else so people aren't hard to find. Some live from hunting or whitebait fishing, others from mining. John and Mark Shaw are gold miners, and although they're retired now they can't resist the urge to sift the sand stirred up by a north-west storm for the flecks of "colour" washed out to the coast.

Gillespies Beach is about twenty kilometres from the Franz Josef Glacier on a wild coast. Beyond piles of driftwood and grassy sand dunes was the shaw's small flat-roofed stone house with tidy lawns, a stone wall is decorated with huge clear-green glass balls, a vegetable garden, a hut, a hen house and a floating duck house. Cooking was done on a wood-fired stove, a generator provided power for the lightbulbs. When we visited the brothers in 1986 their pride and joy was a 1956 Ford Mainline utility. The motor hadn't seen a screwdriver in thirty years. "She's a beauty!" John waved his hand toward a brand new Ford utility that they used to go shopping in Franz Josef.

The Franz Josef Glacier was named by the Austrian Julius von Haast after his emperor back home. The glacier, with its pinnacles, ice needles, crags and crevasses, is certainly majestic and awe-inspiring. At thirteen kilometres in length it is longer than the neighbouring Fox Glacier but by no means the largest in the country. These glaciers draw attention more because of the fact they flow from a height of 2,600 metres almost down to sea level at about 250 metres penetrating into coastal rainforest areas. Glaciers move under enormous pressure from the weight of snow up to 300 metres thick. Westerly winds approaching from the Tasman Sea hit the Southern Alps, forcing the air mass to rise suddenly, producing snow and precipitation. With each snowfall the snow is compacted and at a depth of about twenty metres a refrigerator-blue ice pack forms. These rivers of ice advance and retreat according to climatic conditions. In the 1960s and 1970s the glaciers were retreating but in recent years much excitement has been caused by a steady advance of both the Fox and Franz glaciers, sometimes up to two metres a day!

On the way from Fox Glacier to Gillespies Beach a sign points to Lake Matheson, famous for its perfect mountain reflections. The small lake was formed 14,000 years ago in a depression left by the Fox Glacier as it retreated at the end of the last ice age. The tourist office couldn't have arranged it better because when we visited the reflection was perfect, so good that we put the photo upside down in this book! The deep black waters coloured by algae and humus, and the still morning air allowed a perfect reflection not only of the forest but the Alps and Mt Cook and Mt Tasman. To see this grand panorama requires getting up very early, for even on a windless clear morning the show is limited in time.

From Gillespies Beach we could have taken a footbridge over the lagoon along an old horse track to get to Okarito, but with our campervan we have to take State Highway 6. Lake Wahapo reminds us that in our very first book we wrote that these poor, almost leafless, waterlogged trees were dying. We were wrong. Kahikatea trees love a swampy environment, reaching up to sixty metres high. They were once sought after for their odourless timber ideal for packing material and until 1946 the wood was favoured for butter boxes. A mere two per cent of all New Zealand's kahikatea have survived.

Beyond the lake a narrow asphalt road heads west towards the coast and Okarito. At the height of the gold rush Okarito had a wharf, twenty-five hotels and 1,500 residents. In spite of the dangerous, ever changing sandbank, Okarito was the best

Panorama reflection in Lake Matheson

harbour on the gold coast. Of the old hotels nothing remains, the last one having burnt down in 1957. Just one tiny youth hostel offers bunk beds, and even that was once the school house. The old shop which in 1986 opened three times a week, is now protected and will be renovated. Once thirty-three shops served 800 gold-seekers. "Those that didn't dig, sold grog, and those that dug drank a lot," says a document in the boat house. Today Okarito is home to white herons, and a population of thirty, including retirees, semi-retired gold prospectors, alternative lifestylers, and the writer Keri Hulme.

Talented and successful, Keri Hulme has put Okarito back on the map. In 1986 we met Keri Hulme by chance while we were dining on fresh mussels and whisky with Bill and Judith, her neighbours. A lot of whisky was consumed, because of the quantity of mussels of course, but we had no idea with whom we were boozing. The year before she had been honoured with the Booker Prize for literature. I immediately read *The Bone People* during a few late nights after our visit. The story is about the relationship between a young mute boy, his alcoholic father, and the painter Kerewin. I was confronted with violence, aggression and desperation spun with mythology, poetry, love, frustration and imagery. I couldn't put the book down.

Keri Hulme's ancestors originated from the Scottish Orkney Islands, Lancashire, and the Ngai Tahu tribe. She describes herself as a wanderer between the cultures and races, a te kaihau, or windeater. She searched for

a publisher for many years before it was published, "Change it? Impossible! I'd rather use the paper as a door stop." It was the Christchurch cooperative Spiral that scraped together money for a first edition of 4,000 copies. Today, many readers travel to Okarito searching for the tower house that Kerewin, the central character, lived in. Keri does live in an unusual self-built two-storey timber house. A sign warns "Strange dogs and cats shot on sight" and when not in the mood for visits she allegedly puts out a sign that reads "Piss off!". Fair enough.

From outside, her house looked much like the surrounding homes, but inside the large octagonal room, which is seemingly

held together by bookshelves, serves as both kitchen and study. Why live at Okarito? Coincidence, she says. She happened to be working at the post office in Greymouth and inquired in the pub (where else?) if any Crown Land was being sold in the area. From twenty-three offers for the land her name was drawn out of a box and she bought it before she'd even seen it. Some time later she drove to Okarito, finding the land terribly overgrown with gorse, and slept overnight in her Landrover. Keri knew this was where she wanted to live. Why? The night at the beach, the black sand, the wind and the waves persuaded her to stay. As we were thanking her for her

Keri Hulme at home on the West Coast

time and excellent coffee, she mentioned Bait the current book that she was working on (we're still waiting!).

Maybe the book has something to do with whitebait. These tiny little fishes are a delicacy along the coast. Keri, along with hundreds of other Coasters, lines up alongside river banks with nets hoping to catch these tiny transparent creatures.

We too "caught" whitebait along the coast. State Highway 6 near Fox cuts through a long avenue of tall rimu trees. We parked in front of the only house for miles so that we could photograph the scene. While Karl took photographs, I began talking to Mary, who was only too happy to

interrupt her task of chopping wood. Her husband died two years earlier, so the 70-year-old was living alone in the house. Neighbours ensured she gets a lift into town, otherwise she takes care of herself. The couple originally moved here when the road was being built, and Mary later worked in the kitchen at the Fox Hotel, and sometimes for a farmer gathering sphagnum moss in the forests. At $13 a pound on the Japanese market, moss-gathering was a good source of income.

We eventually started talking about inanga, or whitebait. Mary talked enthusiastically about her special place at a river mouth where she catches the inanga. She

would place a few coloured boards or stones in the water to help her see the transparent two to five centimetre fish – if you're too slow your neighbour's net is ready to catch what you miss. Whitebaiting attracts droves of fans in spring. Had we ever eaten them? Not yet? Mary hurried into her kitchen and dug around in her deep freeze and pulled out a kilogram block of frozen tiny fish with black and yellow eyes. "Here, you can fry these yourselves this evening. Do you know what they charge for a whitebait patty in the hotel? As an entree $7.50!"

Just mention whitebait on the Coast, even if they're deep frozen, and everyone pricks up their ears. "Take an egg, some flour, a pinch of salt and a handful of fish," Bill, the youth hostel warden explained as he was grabbing the frying pan. "Melt the butter and gently fry the mixture. Consume immediately before someone else does."

We head reluctantly north to Hokitika. Prince Charles was here yesterday, the radio announcer boasts. On an old shed a sign depicted the Eiffel Tower, and promised that Café de Paris was ahead. When Hokitika was the gold mining capital of the West Coast, an elegant Café de Paris stood proudly in the main street. The building has long since burnt down. Today's modern version is fitted out with designer furniture, and the owner really is French. "Prince Charles ate here yesterday," whispered the young women at our neighbouring table, and asked the waiter what he ate. For some years now Hokitika has made its name as New Zealand's greenstone capital. Across the road a busload of tourists storms the

Hokitika, greenstone town, West Coast

greenstone factory to watch skilled artisans cutting and polishing greenstone mostly for souvenirs and jewellery.

Further northwards we reached the Pancake Rocks at Punakaiki. Time, wind and water have eroded weak layers between the harder layers on these limestone cliffs above the Tasman Sea, giving the appearance of a stack of wholemeal pancakes (Punakaiki means lying in a heap). Before you reach the cliffs you can hear the pounding of the surf that breaks inside caves and grottos below the cliffs. Don't drive past Punakaiki when there is a westerly storm on, stop and see the magnificent blowholes.

The Pancake Rocks are on the edge of the Paparoa National Park which was created in 1987 after a bitter debate about the future of the lowland forests along this coastline. Now that the forests have been protected, and tracks developed, you can take one of a number of walks from near the park's information centre, as well as seeing the pancake rocks.

In the far north of the West Coast we completed our tour. Some distance north in Golden Bay began the European history of the islands in Pacific. On December 13, 1642 as Abel Janszoon Tasman sailed his frigates *Zeehaen* and *Heemskerck* northwards along the West Coast, the explorer noted in his journal "a land uplifted high."

He named the discovery Staten Landt. At first forgotten, later it became *Nova Zeelandia* or *Niew Zeeland*. New Zealand. ∎

Te Paki sand dunes, Northland

Farm house on the road to Arthur's Pass

Photography

In 1985, when I began taking photographs for our first book on New Zealand I was greatly impressed and inspired by the work of New Zealand photographer Robin Morrison (*South Island From the Road* and *Sense of Place*). The late 49-year-old photographer understood wonderfully how to find and portray people in their typical environment, often in faded and forgotten places. The way in which I portrayed Fred and Myrtle for example was influenced by his art of seeing. Later the work of Andris Apse and Craig Potton, New Zealand's best landscape photographers, encouraged me to extend myself.

In 1985 I arrived in New Zealand with brand new Leica camera equipment and have continued to work with Leica since. I wouldn't want to be without their high quality optics, precise light meters and robust bodies. I seldom work with zoom lenses and most of the time use lenses from 19 mm to 280 mm. My standard lens is a 28 mm wide angle. For long shots I prefer to work with a 180 mm lens.

I only use a tripod in difficult light conditions or when long focal lengths are required, and even then usually a compact table Leica tripod which I can carry in my pocket. My 'light tramping' equipment usually consists of two Leica-RE bodies without winder, pocket tripod, and 19, 28, 90, 180 mm lenses. These pack easily into a comfortable hip bag; without film this weighs about four kilos.

For most foreign visitors New Zealand is a photographer's paradise. The intense light in the Southern Hemisphere highlights the landscape and contours quite vividly. However the extreme contrasts of light and shadows make portraits very difficult. The often discussed ozone hole and New Zealand's clean air results in extremely intense UV-light rays felt not only on the skin but on photographic film. The UV-light produces a noticeable blue tinge, and with differing light refraction, can change the sharpness on the film. Consequently a normal UV filter for sunny weather is not sufficient. Strong skylight filters (e.g. KR 1.5 or 81A) are a must and polarising filters do a good job too.

I often wonder what has happened to all the people I have documented with my camera over the years. Ben for example. He is the young fellow on page 103 with the preying mantis on his nose. Ben was eight-years-old when I first met him in 1983 in a Waldorf School, while working for Ian Athfield in Hastings. Some years later I sent him a calendar from Germany with his portrait, but he never replied. Then in 1994 I looked up his telephone number and gave him a call. The calendar did arrive and still hangs on his bedroom wall, and no, he hadn't forgotten the photographer and gave us a warm welcome. He lives with his mother in a house 'on the beach' and dreams of a trip to Europe...

Thanks!

My special thanks go to Ian and Clare Athfield Wellington. In 1983, during my three-year-journey around the world and my first visit to New Zealand, they gave me a spontaneous and warm welcome, my first job opportunity as a photographer and a home in their living and working labyrinth above Wellington Harbour. Through them and their staff I learned the spirit of New Zealand. And since then their house has been our 'base camp' down under.

Many thanks to my photographer-publisher colleague Craig Potton, his manager Robbie Burton and editor David Chowdhury. Thanks for inspiration and creative collaboration in enabling our German book to be published in New Zealand.

Grateful acknowledgement is made to the following individuals, companies and institutions for supporting this book project: Barbara Ludwig, Petra Lange, Constanze Busch and Jenny Burgess from the New Zealand Tourism Board in Frankfurt; Graeme F. Ching, Kathryn Weir and Debbie Otley from the New Zealand Tourism Board in Wellington; Air New Zealand (for the comfortable flight); and Chris Alpe from Maui Campers. Thanks to the Department of Conservation in Auckland, Brian Mosen from the CCA (Camp and Cabin Association) and New Zealand Rail.

In New Zealand we were always made welcome with enormous hospitality and generosity. Thanks are owed to all the people we met who made our travels, photography and understanding of the country a great pleasure:

Andris and Jenny Apse, Rangiora; Barry Brickell, Coromandel; Ben Chorley, Te Awanga; Judy and Bill Clarkson, Flax Hills, Kaikoura; Rex and Dorothy, Banks Peninsula; Dick Deaker and Jeff Carter, Te Anau; Fred and Myrtle Flutey, Bluff; Leon and Bron Hagenaars, Raglan; Dan Hansen and friends, Wilderland; Keri Hulme, Okarito; Friedensreich Hundertwasser, Bay of Islands; Jack's Place, West Coast (wonderful German bread); John Donna and friends, Ruatoria; Mary Pearse, West Coast; Judith Maloney and Bill Minehan, Okarito; Ray and Lesley Searle (for the long friendship), Auckland; Mark and John Shaw, Gillespies Beach; Ian Snowden, Skip Johnson and their mustering team, Glenaray; Bill Tawhai, Te Kaha; Jo, Biz and the boys, Portobello. Last, but not least, a special thanks to our friend and painter Gus Watson. Whenever we returned to his house and studio in the hills of Dalefield near Queenstown, he impressed and inspired us with his creative energy and his positive spirit.

Foto: Karl-Heinz Raach

Karl Johaentges,
born in Germany 1948

After working for five years in his profession as an architect in Hanover, Karl decided 'now or never' and travelled for three years around the globe, working for architects in Japan, India, Hong Kong, Australia and New Zealand. In 1983 Karl was employed for six months by Ian Athfield in Wellington, mainly to photograph the houses of this imaginative New Zealand architect. It was a job that marked the beginning of his professional career as a photographer.

Back in Germany in 1985 he published his first book *Pictures of a World Trip* and founded a small publishing company. In 1986 he returned with his partner Jackie Blackwood to New Zealand for his following book. Since then KaJo publishers have produced prize-winning German books such as *Pictures from Ireland, Lisbon – Hong Kong by Rail*, and other books on Scotland, USA, Hong Kong, as well as aerial photographic books such as *With a hot air Balloon above Eastern Germany* and *Above Northern Germany*. His photographic essays have appeared in many major German magazines.

Jackie Blackwood,
born in Scotland 1959

Jackie's first long journey began before her second birthday when her parents emigrated to Australia as 'ten pound tourists'. During her university education she worked for two years as a governess on Australian outback stations. Before taking off for her world trip she managed a book shop for three years in Perth. Arriving in Germany from Asia in 1985 she got stuck in Hanover. She works and lives in Hanover and dreams of a little house down under.

Other publications from Craig Potton Publishing include:

Landscape photography:

- *New Zealand Landscapes* by Andris Apse
- *Te Wahipounamu South-West New Zealand World Heritage Area* by Andris Apse
- *Classic Walks of New Zealand* by Craig Potton
- *Above New Zealand* by Craig Potton
- *New Zealand Under the Southern Sky* by Craig Potton
- *Tongariro – A Sacred Gift* by Craig Potton
- *Images From a Limestone Landscape* by Craig Potton and Andy Dennis
- *Offerings from Nepal* by Craig Potton and Lisa Choegyal.

Guidebooks:

- *Nature Watch New Zealand – How to Experience New Zealand's Native Wildlife*
- *A Brief Guide to New Zealand Art and Culture* by Naomi O'Connor
- *New Zealand Whitewater 100 Great Kayaking Runs* by Graham Charles

For more information about these or other books, and our calendar and poster ranges, please contact:

Craig Potton Publishing
P.O. Box 555
Nelson
New Zealand.
Phone: 64 3 548 9009
fax: 64 3 5546 9192
e-mail: info @ cpp.co.nz

CRAIG
POTTON
PUBLISHING

Dusky Sound, Fiordland National Park

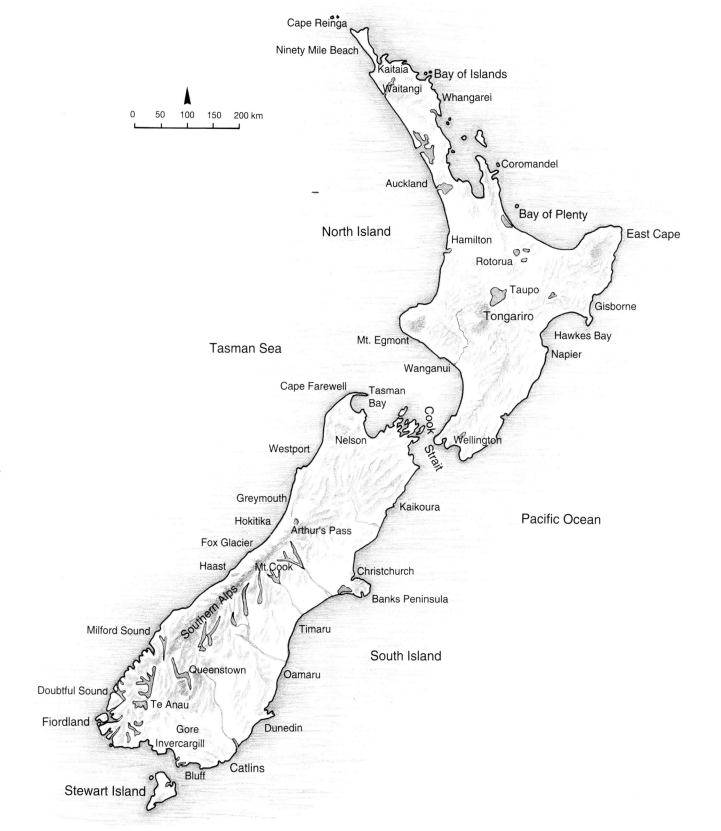

Cape Reinga

Ninety Mile Beach

Kaitaia

Bay of Islands

Waitangi

Whangarei

Coromandel

Auckland

Bay of Plenty

North Island

East Cape

Hamilton

Rotorua

Taupo

Tongariro

Gisborne

Mt. Egmont

Hawkes Bay

Tasman Sea

Napier

Wanganui

Cape Farewell

Tasman Bay

Cook Strait

Nelson

Westport

Wellington

Greymouth

Pacific Ocean

Kaikoura

Hokitika

Arthur's Pass

Fox Glacier

Haast

Mt.Cook

Christchurch

Southern Alps

Banks Peninsula

Milford Sound

Timaru

South Island

Queenstown

Doubtful Sound

Oamaru

Te Anau

Fiordland

Gore

Dunedin

Invercargill

Catlins

Bluff

Stewart Island